FOREWORD by DAMIAN EAD

G000096192

Can thirty seconds really change s
have been thousands upon thousar
crazy and clever enough to volunte.. .... against the
Countdown clock. A clock with just one hand, and one that has given
Mark his own first-hand experience of what it's like to unscramble letters
with a scrambled brain.

Thirty seconds has changed the life of many people. From the millions of
loyal Countdowners the world over, to the participants who have all felt
the blind panic, adrenalin rush and sheer desperation as they hear the
final ticks of that famous old clock.

True, some fair better that others, some enjoy it more than others, but
each have their own very individual and personal tale to tell. From
posting off the application form, to sitting at home waiting for the
programme to start, the very programme they are about to feature in.
Each journey is different, but ultimately the same as all the rest. All about
triumph, disappointment, courage and craft.

For 25 years, Countdown has provided the TV nation with its only real
daily mental work-out. A mind-gymnasium of word searching,
mathematics and conundrum capers. There have been over 4500 editions
of the show, and each one has become a small piece of a giant mosaic.

Thanks for keeping us in the picture.

CRUCIAL! - *A Champion's Tale*

Mark Tournoff

© Mark Tournoff 2007

Crucial! *A Champion's Tale*

ISBN 0-9545072-2-3

Published by Forestdale Publications

24 Cornwall Court

Wilbury Avenue

Hove

Sussex BN3 6GJ

Design & production co-ordinated by:

Fairways Music

Wadebridge

Cornwall

PL27 6BQ

Printed in England

CRUCIAL! - *A Champion's Tale*

Chapter 1: If at first you don't succeed . . .

Few people are lucky enough to realise an impossible dream. For some who are outstanding in their field their goal might be to become Olympic champions, multi-millionaires or 'A' list celebrities. I'm certainly not among them. But I do consider myself privileged, because I discovered an arena in which I could compete with the best. What's more, I had the opportunity to prove it, and had a wonderful time doing so. My endeavours brought a lot of enjoyment to my girlfriend Sue, my family and my friends. Now I want to tell my story so that it will be a source of inspiration to anyone who longs to achieve something memorable, but doubts whether they ever will.

There was no such thing as Countdown when I was growing up in Aldershot, Hampshire during the 1960s and 70s; indeed Channel 4 had yet to grace our television screens. But if someone had set out to design a game that focused on the mental disciplines at which I was strongest, they could hardly have come up with anything more suitable than this test of spelling, vocabulary and arithmetic. English Language - especially the creative-writing aspect - and Mathematics were my favourite subjects at school, and I discovered some talent for other languages, both ancient and modern.

Unfortunately, English Language was not a subject that could be studied at A-level. I did begin A-level Maths but was put off by the discovery that the syllabus content was very different from that of O-level. Where had all the numbers gone, I wondered? Latin was another favourite subject of mine. This was available as an A-level, but not at the school I was attending – Lord Wandsworth College, near Basingstoke. So I ended up taking French, Spanish and Economics. The last of these was definitely a bad choice for me because my experience and understanding of the commercial world was nil. However, I did well enough to be accepted by Exeter University, emerging four years later with a degree in Theology, but no firm idea of what to do with the rest of my life.

It was during my time at Exeter that Countdown became the first programme ever shown on Channel 4, on 2nd November 1982. Based on the French TV programme Des chiffres et des lettres ('numbers and letters'), created by Armand Jammot in 1972, the game pits two contestants against each other in three areas: *letters rounds*, in which they try to make the longest legitimate word from nine randomly selected letters; *numbers rounds*, where they attempt to arrive at a target figure from six given numbers by using basic arithmetic; and a *buzzer round*, which requires them to solve a nine-letter anagram known as a conundrum. I wish I had been among those who witnessed the moment when Richard Whiteley uttered the now famous words: 'As the countdown to a brand new channel ends, a brand new Countdown begins.' Unfortunately, I knew nothing of it at the time. But it wasn't long before I became a regular viewer during the vacations, and I occasionally managed to catch the programme in the common room at university. I used to see what answers I could produce, but didn't actually compete with the contestants or even keep my own score at this stage. At that time Countdown lasted only half an hour, and there were nine rounds instead of fifteen. I always felt this was too short. The preamble, the introductions, the celebrity's contribution and the adverts took up the greater part of the half-hour, leaving only about ten minutes for the game itself.

Soon after graduating I got a job as a VAT inspector in Croydon, before moving into the mundane world of hospital finance. Although the people in Mayday Hospital were pleasant to work with, the job wasn't challenging enough, and I was forever watching the clock to see how long was left before I could go home.

By this time I was watching Countdown regularly. I had made a habit of setting the video and catching up with it in the evenings or at weekends. I was actively competing with the contestants and keeping score. As I frequently won, I concluded that it was time to apply to be on the show. So I called the number given out on the programme, obtained the necessary form and sent it in.

I received an invitation for an audition at a hotel in London. The date in question fell while I was on study-leave to prepare for some exams for the Chartered Institute of Management Accountants (CIMA). On the morning before the audition I was working hard on some complicated subjects. With hindsight this wasn't the ideal prelude to the audition. However, I don't feel that this made a great deal of difference to the outcome. The audition was conducted by the show's producer at that time, Mark Nyman, and there were half a dozen of us in attendance. I actually thought everyone there did really well, but there was one man who seemed to stand out. He appeared to know Mark Nyman through scrabble (of which Mark had recently become World Champion). I felt sure this man would pass the audition, even if the rest of us were unsuccessful - but as far as I know he never appeared on the show. Nor did I ever see any of the others. I still feel mystified that we all fell short of the pass mark. When I received the letter saying that I had not been successful, I naturally felt very disappointed. I knew that Countdown's advice to would-be contestants was not to reapply unless they had very good reason to think they would do better than the previous time. I resolved to try again at some stage; but I decided not to do so until I was so much better that they would have no choice but to let me on the show - even if it took years to reach that stage!

In 1995, at the age of 32, I passed the CIMA exams, and tried to put what I had learned into practice by setting up in business as a promoter and organiser of performances of classical music. This progressed more slowly than I had hoped, and in the end I was forced to conclude that my venture wasn't going to prove viable. I didn't want to go back to the monotony of office work, so I took a driving job working for Business Express, transferring later to Parcelforce, with a view to moving into transport management.

It was around this time that Countdown was extended to fifteen rounds over forty-five minutes. I know not everyone approved of the change, but personally I was delighted. I was still watching every episode of the programme, and making a conscious effort to remember words I had learnt from the contestants or Susie, as well as occasional tips from Carol regarding the numbers games. I was beating the contestants on the show more often than not. But every so often someone of the calibre of record-beater Julian Fell would come along and reinforce my impression that I still wasn't ready to reapply.

It was soon after I moved to Parcelforce that I finally found out what I really wanted to do with the rest of my life. A friend sent me a clipping from a newspaper, on one side of which was a review of a concert we had attended. By chance, I noticed an advert on the other side of the cutting, outlining a course run by The Writing College in Exeter. This course would culminate in a qualification appropriate for freelance editorial work. I made enquiries, but decided it wasn't for me. However, the same college subsequently sent me details of a correspondence course in creative writing. Remembering how I relished this activity at school, I decided to enrol on the course. I found that I enjoyed reading the material and doing the exercises, particularly when the work came back with very positive comments from my tutor. One of the set tasks was to dream up the plot for a novel. What I came up with gripped my imagination so much that I felt compelled to actually write the novel! By now I was nearing completion of the course, so I was soon able to set to work on this enterprise. Within six months I had completed the draft of 'A Nightmare in *Paradise*', and had begun the process of seeking a publisher. I had no misgivings about how difficult this would be. Having received a number of rejection letters from agents and publishers, I decided to self-publish my novel, following the guidance I had received during the course. This meant I would have to decide on the number of copies to be published, and then set about marketing the book myself. Torn between 500 and 1,000, I settled on 800. Compared to the print run of a best seller, it was a tiny number. But for a self-published début novel, the amount seemed daunting. Of one thing I was sure: I must take every opportunity to publicise the book.

It was around this time that I met my girlfriend Sue. I was just about to move to Hove, and, although she lives near Epsom, this did not deter us from getting together. We had both been single for some time, and finding each other made our lives complete. Sue was to become the rock on which I would build my reputation at Countdown. She not only encouraged me to believe I could become a champion, but understood the need to prepare thoroughly and practise hard to achieve this. As a consequence, she waited tolerantly and patiently during the many hours I dedicated to this challenge. Where many people would have grumbled and griped, Sue sustained and supported me through my endeavours, and for this I will never be able fully to express my gratitude.

Some comments Sue made inclined me to think that the time was right to reapply for Countdown. She told me she had never come across anyone who could work with numbers as quickly as I could. She also told me she had mentioned to a friend that I was 'better than most of the people who are actually on the programme'. By now I was getting higher scores than either contestant about 90% of the time, and I felt confident that I was up to the standard required for passing the audition. I was now thinking in terms of whether I could fulfil my growing ambition of becoming overall champion of an entire series.

The main question in my mind was this: how much would I improve if I waited any longer? Might I not be better off applying now, and using the time between the audition and my appearance to concentrate on raising my game even higher. Another factor counted in favour of my applying now. I had sold well over a hundred copies of 'A Nightmare in *Paradise*' in the first few months since publication.

Thereafter the momentum had slackened. It was no worse than I had expected. But it was worse than I had *hoped*. If I wanted the situation to improve, I had to do something about it. An appearance on Countdown, or better still a number of appearances. in which the book was mentioned by name, might just do the trick. I understood that several million people watched Countdown each day. If less than one in a thousand of those people who saw me on the show were inspired to go to their local bookshop and order a copy of 'A Nightmare in *Paradise*' I would sell the remaining copies in one fell swoop. I might even have to think about asking the printer to produce a second print run in order to meet the burgeoning demand. It was too good an opportunity to miss.

Whereas in the days of my first application to Countdown the first stage was to pick up the phone, it was now possible to enquire by email. So I emailed for an application form, which was duly sent. It was an easy form to complete, and it was soon on its way back to Yorkshire. I did not have long to wait before a reply arrived, inviting me for an audition at the Novotel Euston on Tuesday 13th April 2004. The letter explained that the audition would last around 45 minutes and that I would be tested, along with five or six others, on my ability to play the Countdown game. As at my first audition, there would be no scope for influencing the selections of letters or numbers: these would simply be presented to the would-be contestants. Effectively it would be like playing the game at home. The letter was signed by Marie Wale, the programme's Associate Producer, who was to preside over the audition.

In the weeks leading up to the audition I prepared by looking through my dictionary for unfamiliar words. However, the dictionary I owned was not the *Oxford Dictionary of English* (*ODE*), as used for adjudication purposes on the programme. I reasoned that if I passed the audition I would make sure I had the right dictionary for use in preparing for the show. I didn't realise at the time that the *ODE* was so much more comprehensive than the dictionary I was using, otherwise I would have acquired it sooner. With hindsight I was perhaps a little lucky that my ignorance didn't prove to be costly!

The day before the audition was Easter Monday. Sue and I watched that afternoon's episode together at my flat in Hove. I had been doing well against the contestants recently and had put together a decent sequence of 'wins'. But that afternoon I lost! At least it wasn't a heavy defeat. I shrugged it off, and refused to let it affect my belief that I was strong enough to appear on the show.

I travelled by train and tube to Euston and decided to use the time to draw up a short list of words that came up regularly on Countdown, but which did not occur so often in everyday life. One word which came to mind was 'pinafore'. Others included 'tangelo' and 'idolater'.

Normally I turn up for appointments in the nick of time. But as this was something special I made sure I arrived at the hotel very early. I even had time for a cup of coffee before reporting to the reception desk. From there I followed a trail of signs which led to some conference rooms below ground level, where I took a seat in the waiting area. For some time I was the only person there. Eventually a young lady, who seemed very nervous, joined me. I wasn't sure that she was there for the same purpose as me, so I decided not to probe. We sat quietly for a few minutes, until the door to the conference room opened. A lady who introduced herself as

Marie asked us to come in, explaining that as there had been some last-minute cancellations there would be just the two of us. I learned that the other hopeful's name was Joanne, and that this was the first time she had auditioned for Countdown. She asked me whether I had applied before, and I explained how I had been unsuccessful about ten years previously. Marie came across as professional but informal. She chatted pleasantly to us and made us feel at ease. We were encouraged to help ourselves to the coffee, biscuits and soft drinks placed at our disposal.

When the time came to begin, Marie explained the format that would be used to test us: seven letters games, interspersed with three numbers games, and three conundrums at the end. Marie assured us that while the numbers games would not be easy, they were not insoluble. She said that when it came to the conundrums we were to raise our hands to indicate that we had found the answer, but not say what it was until after the thirty seconds had expired, so as not to give it away. Marie pointed out that we weren't competing against each other, but were being assessed against a national standard.

I felt a little apprehensive as Marie began reading out the first set of letters, but as soon as she had finished, my trepidation was replaced by excitement. I had seen a nine-letter word: 'dreamiest'. I sat quietly and tried not to look smug. I hoped that Joanne would see it too, but she had come up with an eight in the shape of 'mastered'. Marie's comment was very encouraging: 'All your years of practice have obviously paid off, Mark.'

From then on I felt increasingly confident that I was going to pass the audition: there were no more opportunities for nine-letter words, but I spotted some eights: 'laxative' was one; 'lemonade', which I had also seen on the previous day's programme, was another. 'Holidays' was one which stood out; and 'pinafore' - one of the words I had listed on the train earlier that morning - also turned up. I did miss a couple of eights: 'autistic' was there (whereas I only saw 'biscuit'), and I could have had 'somewhat', (whereas I struggled to find 'themes').

As for the numbers games, I got two of them spot on, and the third one within three. The solution to the one I missed seemed really obvious when Marie announced it.

When it came to the conundrums, I saw the first two (FAKESMITH = 'makeshift', and ENDPHRASE = 'sharpened') quite quickly. The third conundrum was NOTEPRICE. I considered the ending '-tion', but couldn't rearrange the remaining letters in a meaningful way. It fell to Joanne to reveal that it was, in fact, 'reception'.

Missing the last conundrum was a frustrating conclusion to the audition, but overall I felt I had done well. Later on, I worked out that I had scored 110 out of a possible 126 points. Would this be enough? I knew that I would have to wait for the answer to arrive in the post. But I held on to Marie's comment at the end of the first letters game, and felt that I must have given myself every chance of success.

One further factor gave grounds for optimism. I recalled that at the first audition Mark Nyman had formed a general impression of our ability without noting down every answer. Conversely, Marie had recorded our responses meticulously, so I could be completely confident that her score sheet would be an accurate reflection of my performance at the audition.

As I left the room I thanked Marie and wished her better luck with the attendance for the rest of the day's auditions.

Chapter 2 Game on!

I expected to have to wait some time before the letter containing the outcome of the audition arrived. But just two days later I arrived home to find an envelope bearing the Yorkshire Television stamp. It had to have come from Countdown!

There was some doubt in my mind as to whether the promptness of the response was a good sign. My experience of replies to job applications suggested that it *was*: employers are not slow to contact the successful candidate. But might Countdown be different? Might it be that rejection letters are easier to churn out and therefore come through sooner?

Whatever the answer, I wasn't about to waste any time finding out. I ripped the envelope open, tugged the letter free and scanned it for one of those key words that render the rest of the text superfluous.

'Delighted' was the first word that stood out. It could only mean one thing! I literally jumped for joy before reading the rest of the letter. It was signed by Marie, and was dated 14th April 2004, the day after the audition. The critical paragraph read: 'I am delighted to inform you that your audition was successful and we will be writing to you again over the coming months with details of your recording date.'

As soon as I had finished reading the letter I shared the exciting news with Sue by sending her a text. Her reply confirmed that she had never been in any doubt that I would pass the audition, and that Countdown should 'watch out'! My mother's reaction was different: she was horrified to learn that I was going to appear on the programme! She found the idea of having to perform in such a public arena too daunting, and was concerned that I would be disappointed if it didn't go well. My father's reaction was more positive. And my grandmother, who lives with my parents in Cornwall, and with whom I had often watched Countdown when on vacation from university, was likewise pleased at the news. It caused quite a stir at work as well. A couple of my colleagues got in the habit of humming the closing notes of the theme tune (the bit that goes *da-dum, da-dum, da-da-da-dum*) whenever our paths crossed!

There followed some weeks of waiting for news of the recording date. At this point in time series 51 was being screened, with the finals scheduled for June. Marie had said at the audition that they were looking for contestants for series 52, so I expected it to be a while before I heard anything more.

While visiting my parents, Sue and I took the opportunity to go to the local bookshop, and managed to find the *Oxford Dictionary of English*. I knew when I saw the size of it that I was going to have plenty of work to do before my appearance on the show, and I resolved to make a start right away. The performances of Stewart Holden which culminated in victory in the final of series 51 left me in no doubt that I could not afford to relax my efforts if I wanted to become the next series champion.

I remember watching one particular episode with Sue, and feeling disappointed at the number of words I had either not seen or not known. I told Sue that I simply had to get better at the game. At the start of series 52, David Thirlwall took up where he had left off at the end of the previous series, and went on to become an 'octochamp', or 'octavian' (Countdown's alternative words for a contestant who wins the maximum of eight games), notching up a total of 704 points. My record against David was encouraging: six wins and a tie, with just one defeat. Each day from then on as I watched Countdown I was looking out for other major contenders to show up. At that time the next day's contestant would sit in the 'hot seat' at the front of the audience. This would give them a feel for what it was like to be on the set. Richard Whiteley would introduce them at the end of the programme, and ask one or two questions, such as whether they had solved the conundrum. When one day in August I saw Jack Welsby in the hot seat, I sensed that a serious pretender to the title had arrived on the scene. It was obvious that Jack was intelligent. Moreover, Richard mentioned that there was a particular achievement about which he would like to know more when Jack appeared the next day. Jack looked puzzled as to what Richard might want to ask him about. It turned out that Jack held the world record for having travelled through every London underground station in the shortest time. But Jack's uncertainty was understandable: he had also been overall series champion of Channel 4's general knowledge quiz, Fifteen to One.

Jack soon showed that he had considerable ability at Countdown. He overhauled the previous day's champion, John Stitcher - despite missing the nine-letter word, 'dislocate', which his opponent spotted. I too saw 'dislocate', but that would not have sufficed for me to beat Jack either. Predictably, Jack went on to become an octavian, and at that stage was clearly the person everyone would have to beat. I managed just two wins against him. His prowess in the numbers games, in which he always opted for 'six small numbers', was remarkable, but he also came up with some excellent words, such as 'landties' and 'buddleia'.

At this point I was still waiting for a recording date, and I began to wonder whether I might hope to be given a slot in the next series instead, so that I wouldn't have to come up against Jack. But I knew that there would be outstanding players in every series, and if I didn't have to play Jack I might well come up against another 'ace'. The answer was to carry on practising and enhancing my vocabulary until I could compete with the best of them. In any case, I felt curiously certain that I *was* going to come up against Jack, and that whoever won the duel would be the champion of the series.

Some weeks went by without anyone staying in the champion's chair for very long. Towards the end of the summer, an Irish contestant named Roy Thirle was putting together a sequence of wins, when along came his compatriot Paul Gallen. It didn't begin well for Paul, as he failed to score in either of the first two rounds. But thereafter he got going, eventually notching up 96 points on the way to victory. On that day I would have won by a single point. But in the process of becoming the third octavian of the series Paul would have beaten me in four of the other seven games. Paul went on to overtake Jack's total of 831 points to become number one seed with 846 points. It was clear that there was another serious contender for the title of series champion.

At the start of September I had still heard nothing more about my recording date, and wanted to know whether I would need to set aside some of my remaining annual leave for a trip to Yorkshire. So I rang the Countdown studio to ask if they could tell me when I was likely to be called up. I learned that there were still some slots available for the current series, and I would be hearing more in the very near future. Sure enough, a few days later a letter arrived from the programme's researcher, Charlotte Hudson, asking me to come to the studio on 13th October.

In my letter confirming my acceptance of the invitation I mentioned how much I was looking forward to taking part in the show. I returned the form Charlotte had sent, disclosing details that Richard could use when I was introduced: favourite music, sporting interests, hobbies, and so on. In the 'ambitions' section I said that I wanted to pursue my writing activities on a full-time basis. In the letter to Charlotte I added that 'my first novel, entitled "A Nightmare in *Paradise*", was published last year and is available through any major bookshop. If it is at all possible to mention this when I am introduced I would be most grateful, as it may be conducive to realising my ambition.'

The letter of acceptance was dated 13th September 2004. I had exactly one month in which to prepare for my appearance. In the meantime, one more serious contender emerged in the form of John Gray. Like David Thirlwall before him, John worked for the Department of Customs and Excise. John also went on to become an octavian, the fourth so far in series 52. My record in John's games was good: I would have won six out of eight. By the end of his run John had amassed 757 points to become number three seed.

During September I took a week off work to spend time at home preparing for my impending appearance. Fortunately, the weather was warm and sunny, and I was able to sit out on the balcony, from where I have a good view of Hove and a distant glimpse of the sea. I worked through the dictionary methodically, compiling lists of words, according to suffix, origin or other distinctive feature. I found this an interesting task - although I would have preferred not spending quite so much time on it as I did, if I could have achieved the same results! The more I looked through the dictionary, the more I realised how much there was to know. However, I wasn't put off; I wanted to give it all I could. I knew that there was a real chance that it would make a vital difference to the outcome of my quest to become champion of the series.

By this time I was making good use of a technique I had come up with for practising conundrums. You will find details of how to work with 'squares' in the final section of this book: basically it involves using pocket-sized pieces of paper with conundrums on one side and the answers on the other. Sue helped me with my preparations by making up conundrums, which she would send me by text on a daily basis. I would try to do these as quickly as I could, and text back the answer, together with a note of approximately how long it had taken me. If I didn't see them straight off, I would concentrate hard for thirty seconds or so. If I hadn't solved them by then, I continued to look at them for perhaps another minute, and if I was still struggling after that I would put them aside and come back to them periodically. One word which left me completely flummoxed was 'incubator'. And I remember that it took me well over a day to come up with 'nostalgia'!

I made an important discovery as a result of this practice. If I didn't see the answer within a few seconds, I would greatly increase my chances of doing so if I wrote the letters down in the form of a 'grid' (three rows of three letters), just as I would if it were a normal letters game. This practice used up about ten seconds, but it tended to make the answer fall into place. It occurred to me at this point that the technique might come in useful if I were faced with a crucial conundrum. I resolved that I would definitely use it following an incorrect guess by my opponent, if I were given sufficient time to do so.

I also did quite a bit of practice for the numbers games. This included looking at target numbers analytically, so that it became second nature to notice that a three-digit number was divisible by, say, eleven, or thirty-seven. It occurred to me that it would be useful to recognise targets which could be reached directly by multiplying two two-digit prime numbers by each other, (e.g. $703 = 19 \times 37$). So I compiled a list of such combinations and tried to memorise them. This proved very difficult, and, although I didn't make a conscious decision to stop, I couldn't say that I ever got to the stage where I knew the list well.

One enjoyable aspect of the preparation was the trip to Marks and Spencer to buy the shirts I would have to take to Leeds. Every contestant is asked to take eight different tops, to allow for the possibility of appearing in the maximum number of shows. There were guidelines to follow: shirts with patterns or checks should be avoided, and bold colours were considered preferable to pale ones. I decided I had just one shirt in my wardrobe which would look good on the show, and would therefore have to get seven new ones. I reasoned that even if I didn't need them all for Countdown, I would make use of them socially. Sue helped me choose a selection of blue, maroon and lilac - colours that we felt would blend well with the striking tones of the Countdown set.

The last few days leading up to the recording date are something of a blur. I was very focused on the task that lay ahead, and excited about the thought of taking part in the show. During one conversation with my parents Sue revealed that she was feeling a lot more nervous about it than I was, and this became something of a standing joke. I was determined to keep the inevitable apprehension under control, so that it didn't detract from my performance.

Chapter 3: 'It's like meeting up with old friends!'

We drove to Leeds on Tuesday 12th October, the day before the recording date. By following the instructions we had been sent we arrived at the Holiday Inn Express, where Countdown contestants are lodged at the programme's expense. At that time the hotel provided breakfast only, so we chose from the variety of takeaway menus and ordered our evening meals, which were delivered to the hotel. After we had eaten in the bar area we enquired as to the whereabouts of the Yorkshire TV studios and discovered that they were straight down the road, just a few minutes' walk away. After a relaxing drink, we had an early night, and slept well.

The big day finally arrived. At breakfast we looked around to see who among the other guests looked the 'type' to be on Countdown. But everyone we saw looked like business people. Arriving at the studio in good time, we reported to reception, where we were asked to take a seat while waiting to be shown to the Countdown studio. Now we surely were among other contestants, although there must have been a few people who were waiting there for other reasons.

It wasn't long before a young lady appeared, introduced herself as Lisa, and asked cheerfully who had come for Countdown. Once Lisa had established our identities, and those of our guests, she escorted us through the security door and into the corridor leading to the Countdown studio. Along this corridor were the dressing rooms, make-up rooms, and the Green Room. This was to be the contestants' base: it was comfortable and well equipped with refreshments (tea, coffee, fruit and chilled water). We met Charlotte, with whom I had corresponded, and whose role encompassed assisting Lisa backstage. Like Lisa, Charlotte came across as a good organiser with a lively personality. Our first impressions of Countdown behind the scenes were encouraging. The welcome from the staff was warm and friendly, and our surroundings helped us to feel at ease.

I had expected to be taking part in the second show of the day. However, we soon learned that the final show of the previous day's recordings had seen another contestant (Steve Moir) become an octavian. This meant that there was no reigning champion from the previous day. This was welcome news. I had prepared for the possibility of having to take on a multiple champion on my début. Now I would be spared this: instead I would take part in the first show of the day, alongside another player with no previous experience. Five shows (a week's worth of Countdown) were to be recorded that day. The rest of the day's contestants were also moved forward one show, and a competitor who had been placed on standby was called up.

My opponent in the opening game was to be Margaret Boyle, a retired Scottish lady who now lived in Hertfordshire. Charlotte tossed the coin which determined who sat in which chair: I won the toss and chose to sit in the challenger's chair.

The rest of the time before the show was taken up with preparations. Charlotte ran through the personal details we had provided for the profiles that Richard would use at the start of the show. Our outfits were checked for suitability by Helen from the costume and make-up department. My collection of new shirts was awarded an instant seal of approval. We went to our respective dressing rooms to change; then we were shown to the make-up room. There was a surprise in store at this point: Carol Vorderman and Susie Dent were in the room, being made up at the same time as us. Although I knew that they were essentially down-to-earth people who weren't obsessed with their celebrity status, it hadn't crossed my mind that they would share a make-up room with the contestants!

I was still registering my surprise when Carol said 'Hello'. It felt quite easy, exchanging pleasantries with someone so famous, because I had watched Countdown for so long that I felt as though I already knew Carol well. The same applied to Susie and Richard. I mentioned to Carol during our brief conversation in the make-up room that 'It's like meeting up with old friends!' Carol was just the same behind the scenes as she is on the show: chatty, vivacious and good-humoured. Although I didn't have much chance to speak to Susie at this point, she immediately came across as the warm and sensitive person I knew from watching the show.

The time to make our way to the studio soon came. Sue had to go first, as the contestants wait until the audience is assembled before taking their places. She gave me a hug and a good-luck kiss before following Lisa down the corridor. Lisa soon came back for Margaret and me, and those remaining in the Green Room wished us well as we too set off along the corridor. The door through which we entered the studio was located at the other end of the room from the set, near the tiers of seats where the studio audience sits. There was a warm-up act in progress: a comedian named Dudley was entertaining the audience, telling amusing stories and making witty observations in a thick northern accent. Lisa led us past the audience, and we made our way through a gap between the board on which the conundrum is displayed and several cameras positioned on that side of the room. After showing us to our seats, Lisa went over the procedure for checking our words and calculations. I was to show mine to Richard, whereas Margaret was to pass hers to the celebrity in Dictionary Corner, who on this occasion was Jeremy Beadle.

The sound technician came along with our microphones, which we had to thread under our clothing and attach to our tops at the neckline. He then performed a sound check, by asking us either to count to ten or to tell him what we had for breakfast. The final touches were applied to our make-up, and at last we were ready for action.

Chapter 4: On the road to success . . .

Richard Whiteley took his place, and we exchanged greetings. On this occasion Richard seemed a little more serious and subdued than he usually was on the show. He

25

looked through my profile, and remarked on the fact that I had written a novel. I told him that I was hoping to mention it by name, and he said that he would ask me about it. This encouraged me to feel that the venture was going to be worthwhile, whether I won or lost.

The floor manager, Annie, signalled the go-ahead for the programme to begin. As the Countdown theme tune was played, the audience was encouraged to clap and cheer. I took deep breaths and looked down at the monitor, which is set in the desk in front each contestant. The screen showed Carol, looking cheerful as she stood over by the numbers board in readiness for the start of the show. I found that watching Carol looking so serene aided my attempts to stay calm and relaxed. Also the layout and the lighting on the set were helpful in this respect. Everything in the immediate vicinity was bright and vivid, whereas the cameras and the audience seemed to recede into the distance. It created a cosy atmosphere, which made it easier to treat the whole experience light-heartedly, and to imagine that I was simply playing along at home, as I had done while watching so many hundreds of episodes.

Richard was soon in full flow, telling one of the jokes that only Richard can tell. This was interspersed with the usual banter with Carol. When the time came to introduce the contestants, Richard began with me. Reading directly from my profile, he started by saying that I was divorced. I wished I had thought to ask Charlotte to remove any mention of my marital status from the profile. It wasn't something I wanted to proclaim to the world! Happily Richard moved quickly on to say that I was a driver for the Royal Mail, but that I was also a novelist, and that my ambitions were to write full-time, and live to the age of one hundred. He then fulfilled his promise to ask me what my novel was called. I replied proudly and with a sense of triumph that it was called 'A Nightmare in *Paradise*.' Richard went on to identify my favourite book as *Lord of the Rings*. He must have seen the surprised look on my face, because he promptly corrected this to *Lord of the Flies*, before reeling off some corny puns which had been scripted for him about buzzing into the studio and swatting my opponent!

It was Margaret's turn to be introduced. She seemed very nervous. She told me afterwards that it was the mention of my being a writer which unnerved her. This was obviously on her mind during the opening rounds. Once Richard had introduced Jeremy Beadle the game was finally under way. As Margaret was sitting in the champion's chair, it fell to her to make the first selection of letters.

I noted each of the letters carefully as they came out: M R E O L T J A U. Richard pressed the button to start the clock. The music came over loud and clear. I didn't find it intrusive, as I am well practised at relegating it to my subconscious. I think I'm right in saying that the sound comes from behind you, but the fact that I'm not sure illustrates how effectively I shut it out!

I spotted the six-letter word 'morale' fairly early on in the thirty seconds, but struggled to improve on this. Just before time ran out, I thought I had managed one better. I hastily scribbled down '*tremulo*'[*] and declared a seven. Even as I

---

[*]*To avoid misleading readers, words which are not acceptable on Countdown are in italics.*

spoke I realised my mistake: as Susie explained, I had muddled 'tremolo' with 'tremulous'. It turned out that Margaret's word '*jolter*', was not listed in the dictionary, leaving the scores at 0:0 after round one.

This was not how I had envisaged starting out on my quest, but I knew it was important to shrug it off and set about making amends. My first choice of letters enabled me to get off the mark with 'opines'. As Margaret had declared a five, in the form of 'yawns', it was sufficient to enable me to take the lead. However, Susie pointed out that we could have had the seven-letter word 'weapons'.

The outcome of round three was similar: I had 'cubist' for six, edging out Margaret's five-letter word 'crabs'. Richard sounded very impressed with my word, which he repeated enthusiastically. But we could have had a seven with the seemingly improbable 'upstair'. It wasn't until round four that I finally produced a word which could not have been bettered, in the form of 'atomised'. Margaret was again one letter behind me, having seen 'mastoid'.

The numbers game which followed involved an awkward target of 838. I arrived at 839 by the same method as Carol; much later I worked out that it was possible to get the target exactly, by a rather obscure method. Margaret was further away on 828. I felt a bit uncomfortable about the fact that I kept doing slightly better than her, and that as a result I had reached 27 points with Margaret yet to score.

Jeremy Beadle then came up with some really interesting little-known facts about Richard Whiteley, prefacing each by seeking - and obtaining - confirmation that it was true. For example, Jeremy noted that Richard was the most seen face on British television, that he had been taught by Russell

Harty, and that he still had his old tuck-box from his schooldays.

During the break Richard gave some words of encouragement to Margaret, assuring her that she would soon get off the mark. Margaret didn't seem convinced; but in the very next round she notched up seven points with 'oranges', a score which I matched with 'nosebag'. There were several words which you only had to mention to make Richard chuckle, and 'nosebag' turned out to be one of them.

We both spotted 'cloaked' in round seven, taking the score on to 41:14. In the next round I produced 'maltier' for seven points, while Margaret came up with the unacceptable 'retile'[*]. An awkward selection in the next round meant that neither of us got past the five-letter word 'foams'.

As I now held enough of a lead to feel confident that I was going to win the game, I began to concentrate on maximising my score, in the hope of amassing sufficient points to overtake Paul Gallen. I had worked out that if I could achieve this both Paul and Jack would be in the other half of the draw for the quarter-finals, and there would be no question of having to play both of them.

With this in mind my first numbers selection was 'one from the top and five small numbers' - the combination most likely to yield maximum points. The target was 726. I saw how to make 725 straight away: $(10 \times 75) - (5 \times 5)$. I spent almost the entire thirty seconds vainly trying to make 24 from 5, 5, 4, and 2, with a view to subtracting this figure from the 750 produced by the first part of the equation.

---

[*] Note that I have not italicised this word as it has now found its way into the *ODE*.

As it was, we both scored 7 points for arriving at 725, Margaret's calculations being identical to mine. Carol revealed that there was a very easy way of getting the maximum points: $(75 - 2) \times 10 = 730$, less 4 = 726. When I saw Carol point this out, it seemed blatantly obvious, and I was dismayed that I had failed to spot it! I also knew that I might not be lucky enough to get away with it if I were to miss something like that against an arithmetic specialist like Jack Welsby.

At the start of the third part of the programme (or as Richard would say, 'the third half'), I led by 60 points to Margaret's 26. I was still hopeful that I might score a century on my debut. What happened in the next letters game made it very unlikely that I would do. Margaret came up with 'hardiest', beating my 'shorted' to claim eight points. As with the numbers game which had preceded the interval, when I looked again I couldn't believe my oversight! Had I become a little complacent from the extent of my lead? Or was I more affected by the occasion than I realised? I still don't know.

At the start of the next round Richard decided with his usual unfathomable quirkiness to call me 'Marco'. I interpreted it as an indication that he had taken a liking to me.

We tied the game which followed with sevens: I saw 'cordage', while Margaret declared 'groaned'. But everyone - including Susie - missed 'renegado'. The last letters game produced a miserable selection, and was also tied with the five-letter word 'quote'. Susie drew our attention to an obscure six, in the form of 'cloque' (a fabric with an irregularly raised or embossed surface).

The scores had moved on to 76:46. There followed an amusing moment as Richard turned to me and told me it was my choice of letters. I corrected him politely: 'Numbers,' I said. As I knew the game was safe, I again asked for 'one large number and five small ones'. Again there was an easy means of arriving at the target, and this time I saw it straight away. I was able to claim maximum points in a numbers game for the first time, and was able to relax for the remainder of the thirty seconds. Unfortunately for Margaret, she didn't spot the solution.

The time had come for my first experience of a Countdown conundrum. It was the element of the game I had always thought the most daunting. Not only are you working against the clock; you are also trying to react more quickly than your opponent, as only the contestant who first solves the conundrum will score any points.

Richard instructed us to put our fingers on our buzzers. These are round silver knobs about the size of a fingertip, with a circular surround. They are set into the desk and can only be reached by having your right arm fully outstretched, presumably to stop contestants pressing them by accident during the show.

Once Richard had established that we were both ready he asked for the conundrum to be revealed. FIENDFEST appeared on the monitor. It didn't immediately fall into place. However, I felt fairly sure the two 'f's would belong together, and this enabled me to piece together the word 'stiffened' after about ten seconds. I pressed the buzzer, in so doing giving myself something of a start, as the sound was louder than I had expected! Richard confirmed that I had solved my first conundrum correctly.

It took our scores on to 92:46. Looking back, I was not that impressed with my own performance. I only achieved the maximum available score in six of the fifteen rounds.

Margaret was very sporting, and was more disappointed because she hadn't played as well as she might have done than because of the outcome of the game. Sue spent some time with her as the day went by, and helped keep her spirits up.

At the end of the show we were asked to do some very short retakes. These appeared to be mainly for the purpose of enabling the show to be curtailed slightly, so that it didn't exceed its allotted time. There was very little that needed to be redone as a consequence of not being up to scratch, the whole show having been conducted in a very slick manner, as might be expected from the level of experience of those involved.

There was about half an hour between the end of this show and the start of the next, which meant that all those who would be returning had to go to their dressing rooms to change their clothes. Those who remained seated throughout the shows needed only to change their tops, but as Carol appears in a standing position this entailed a completely different outfit each time.

My next opponent was to be Brian Pulman, an entertainer. Sue had been sitting in the audience near Brian, who had been in the 'hot seat' in preparation for his appearance. Brian had asked her whether I was as good at home, and Sue had told him that I was. Realistically, I would have expected to do better than that at home. I hoped that my sub-standard performance was just down to unfamiliarity with the situation, and that I would settle in and give an improved display against Brian.

We were soon back in the studio: this time I moved across to the champion's chair, which meant that I was sitting next to Jeremy Beadle. Although I had seen You've Been Framed occasionally, I didn't feel as though I knew Jeremy to the extent that I knew the Countdown regulars. Nevertheless, I found Jeremy very down-to-earth and easy to chat with: he was interested in my writing, and had a very encouraging attitude towards the contestants. I told him about the occasion when I had been doing some overtime on parcel delivery, and had visited a Surrey address with a parcel for one 'Jeremy Beadle', who was not at home. Of course, I had wondered whether I might have met him then (I had come across Michael Crawford and Lynne Truss in this manner). However, Jeremy said that he lived elsewhere.

The game got under way with my choice of letters: the seven-letter word 'mothers' stood out. Brian spotted this too. Susie pointed out that we could have had 'theorems'. From Brian's first selection I came up with 'miscue', which Brian equalled with 'exacts': again we might have done better: Susie revealed that 'caesium' was there for seven.

In round three we both got 'spooked', taking the scores on to 20:20. Brian's next selection proved difficult, and we managed just fives between us: I saw 'mogul', while Brian declared 'guilt'. I was really disappointed to discover from Susie that we could have had 'agouti' for six. When discussing Countdown with people, I have often mentioned that there are various words which come up regularly on the programme, but which rarely crop up elsewhere: along with 'gherao', 'agouti' is one of the words I cite by way of illustration of this point!

I decided to try to break the deadlock with a testing numbers game, and asked for 'three large ones and three small ones'. A target of 357 did indeed prove awkward, and for most of the thirty seconds I was struggling. I had seen a way of making 350, but couldn't find the extra 7. Towards the end it occurred to me that I could make 375, and work downwards. With just a couple of seconds to spare I realised I could multiply 9 by 2 to arrive at the 18 I needed to subtract in order to hit the target. It was too late to write anything down: moreover, I suddenly realised I couldn't remember how I had used the remaining numbers to make 375! Immediately Richard asked for my declaration, and I was faced with a dilemma. Should I risk trying to recall all my calculations? I really wanted the ten points that I felt my endeavours had merited, and decided to risk declaring 357. Brian was 5 away: if I could remember the first part of the equation I would be ahead.

I looked again: suddenly it was obvious that I had multiplied 6 by 50, and added the 75. I was confident about the remainder of the calculation, and was very relieved that I was able to claim a ten-point lead at the end of the first 'half' of the game.

Before the interval Jeremy Beadle carried on where he had left off the previous day with some more interesting facts about Richard. He mentioned that Richard had once been voted 'Wet leak of the year' by the 'Starter for ten group', that his role model was David Frost, and that he had been the star of a Japanese beer advertisement.

Round six saw another tied letters game: Brian and I both saw 'brained' for seven points. Susie produced a surprising alternative in 'unfired' (relating to a gun or pottery).

It was only in round seven that a letters game went my way. I managed to see the eight-letter word 'apricots', while Brian (rather appropriately) saw 'actors'. My lead stretched to 25 points in the next round through 'gadroon', a word which I knew from my painstaking perusal of the dictionary. When Richard asked whether I knew what it meant, I admitted that I had no idea, but I had remembered the word because I liked the sound of it. Brian must have been a bit miffed: he had seen 'dragon', whereas he could have equalled my word by inserting an 'o' to make 'dragoon'. We tied the next round with 'wanders' and 'wardens' for sevens, but there were a couple of eights which got away: 'answered' and 'undersea'.

Brian asked for one large number and five small ones. The target of 567 was tricky, but I found a way of getting 569. I was closer than Brian, and so extended my lead to 32 points. It had been a good 'half' of the programme for me: the game had gone from being very close to being heavily weighted in my favour.

After the interval we tied the first letters game with 'plague'. Susie came up with a great seven in the form of 'pigface' (an Australian plant). The eight-letter word 'inverted' stood out in round twelve, and the points were shared.

So far I had scored in every round. But Brian put an end to that in the final letters game, spotting 'imitates', to better my 'atheism'. By this time I was far enough ahead for it not to matter, and I would still be able to notch up my first century if I scored in the last two rounds.

A target of 396 from Brian's second choice of numbers didn't prove too difficult for either of us. Only the conundrum remained. Richard reminded us to put our fingers on our respective buzzers, and LOGBEHIND appeared on the screen. It was one of those conundrums you dream about, when you see the word straight away and are in no doubt that you are right. It might as well have said 'beholding'. Brian saw it too, but I was quicker on the buzzer. The sound of the champion's buzzer was different from that of the challenger's, and it gave me even more of a start! 'It made me jump!' I exclaimed.

Richard confirmed that I had solved the conundrum correctly. It took the final scores on to 105:71. Graciously, Brian said that he didn't mind losing to a 'centurion'.

Sitting in the 'hot seat' for that show was Ronnie Boyd, who hailed from Paisley. Richard asked his opinion of the performance he had just seen.

'He's good,' Ronnie acknowledged in a broad Scottish accent.

'But are *you* good?' Richard wanted to know. 'Hopefully,' said Ronnie.

I expected a serious challenge from Ronnie. We had discussed our auditions earlier in the day: Ronnie recalled seeing the nine-letter word 'culminate' at his, which I thought quite impressive. And it's well known that Scotland produces more than its fair share of impressive Countdown players. However, I hadn't reckoned with what happened in the very first round of our match . . .

As the reigning champion, it had fallen to me to make the first choice of letters. A promising looking selection emerged: however, I couldn't get past the six-letter word 'rancid'. I felt sure there was something longer, and expected to hear that Ronnie had at least a seven. But when Ronnie was asked to declare, he said quite calmly:

'Nine.'

There was a gasp of admiration from the audience. I sat stunned, wondering what Ronnie had spotted. Richard asked Ronnie for his word. 'Manicured,' was his reply.

I felt annoyed with myself for missing this word. It wasn't the first time I had failed to see 'manicured'. I recalled missing it during a game that had taken place during the preceding series.

An eighteen-point deficit right at the start of the contest was the nightmare scenario! Sue says that she didn't despair at this point. She knew that I would look upon it as a challenge and that I would rise to it. If I had been asked there and then whether I would settle for taking the game to a crucial conundrum I would have said 'yes'. The answer would have been even more emphatic, had the question been posed immediately after we had made our declarations at the end of the second round. From a trickier selection I had managed a mere five-letter word, 'skate', whereas Ronnie stated that he had seen a six.

Was I about to crash out of Countdown in spectacular style? If Ronnie's word were confirmed as being valid I would be 24:0 down! Susie checked '*slatey*', then told Ronnie apologetically that it wasn't there. I registered my first five points and the gap narrowed to thirteen. Susie pointed out that 'stalky' would have been allowed. We could also have had 'koalas' for six points.

It was down to me to choose some more letters. The suffix '-head' came to mind as my selection took shape. Almost as soon as the ninth letter was in place the word 'printhead' leapt out at me! I knew it was definitely in the dictionary because I had seen it there during my preparation. I was certain it wasn't hyphenated. Moreover, I had identified it as a high probability nine-letter word and included it on the material I used for practice (more on that later). I was in no doubt that I had seen my first 'nine'. And with a thirteen-point deficit to overcome, it could hardly have come at a better time!

My immediate reaction was to sit bolt upright and take a sip of water. Then I realised that this would make it obvious that there must be a 'nine' in the selection, so I reverted to my normal stance. I was curious to know whether Susie had spotted 'printhead' as well, and at one point I glanced discreetly in the direction of Dictionary Corner, without getting a concrete idea either way. This moment was captured by one of the cameras and made it into the televised version of the show. I hope nobody thought I was trying to cheat!

When Richard asked for our declarations my 'Nine' brought another gasp from the audience. It was a winner: Ronnie had a seven-letter word, 'painter'. Richard clearly appreciated the significance of this moment. 'Hey, what a game this is!' he remarked. A couple of minutes after I had contemplated the possibility of going 24 points behind, I had taken a five-point lead!

In the following round I spotted a seven-letter word, 'anxious', which everyone else, including Susie, missed. So now I had put some daylight between my score and Ronnie's total. The first numbers game proved no problem for either of us. At the end of part one I led by 40 points to 28.

It wasn't long before I extended my advantage: 'declares' was a winning eight in round six, while in round seven 'reading' was sufficient to take the points after Ronnie had '*pearing*' disallowed.

The middle section of the programme continued to go well for me: I spotted 'duration' to claim the points in round eight. For the second time in the game Susie acknowledged that I had surpassed her efforts. Richard remarked that I was 'becoming something of a beast'. It was his usual way of referring to a player of a good standard, so I was very pleased to hear him say this. In round nine the word 'outreach' was sufficient to add another eight points to my advantage, being one letter longer than Ronnie's 'outrage'.

It was Ronnie's choice of numbers. He asked for '2 large numbers and 4 small ones', and a target of 170 looked likely to be achievable. I was working on what looked like a promising line of thought when an intermittent buzzing sound from above caught my attention. Something was interfering with the sound system. I learned the explanation during the interval which followed, when Susie remarked: 'That mobile phone put you off, didn't it?' It certainly distracted me, and presumably Ronnie too. Although there were several easy solutions, neither of us managed to spot any of them. I was 'one above', whereas Ronnie was 'one below', and seven points were added to each of our scores.

In the letters game which followed the break there were (most unusually) two 'b's in the selection. The word 'tabbies' stood out as the safe option, although 'gabbiest' sounded familiar. I decided not to risk the latter. Ronnie, however, was sure of it, and claimed eight points. It transpired that 'gabby' is another word for 'talkative'.

I won the next round with a 'six', in the form of 'mauver'. Before the first show, I had run through a list of queries with Damian Eadie, the series producer. Damian had first appeared on the show as a contestant, going on to be overall champion of series 28. One of my questions related to the guidelines that Countdown issues to contestants regarding acceptability of comparatives and superlatives. The guidelines indicated that there was no need for these to be specified in respect of single-syllable adjectives. I had wanted to know whether this was always so, even if the word concerned was most unlikely. By a strange coincidence, the word I had given by way of example was 'mauver'. Damian had confirmed that it was an acceptable word. As a result, I was able to declare it with confidence, when otherwise I wouldn't have risked it.

The last letters game was tied with seven-letter words: I saw 'trefoil', while Ronnie came up with 'profile'. I had already done enough to make the game safe before the final numbers game, in which we both arrived at the target of 358. It took my score to 101 points, while Ronnie's moved on to 60.

The conundrum remained. RAINCLIPP appeared on our monitors. Immediately I felt confident that the solution would begin with the letter 'p'. But the presence of a second 'p' at the end of the conundrum threw me for a few seconds. Suddenly, however, it fell into place. I pressed the buzzer - for once managing to avoid startling myself - and identified the word as 'principal'.

Richard was very complimentary about the fact that I had come back from 18:0 down at the end of round one, to win by 51 points. In terms of maximum scores, it was a better performance than either of the first two: I had managed to spot eleven maximums out of fifteen. My reward was an appearance in the fourth show to be recorded that day. My opponent would be Samantha Latham, an Online Learning Coordinator from Wiltshire, who introduced herself to us as 'Sam'.

All the contestants then gathered around the set with Richard, Carol, Susie and Jeremy for a group photo, copies of which were subsequently sent out to us, as a souvenir of our visit to the studio.

There followed a tea break; during this time Sam implied several times that she didn't expect to be taking part in more than one show. I tried to persuade her that she should be more optimistic about her chances. Indeed, when the game got under way it promised to be a close contest. We tied the first letters game with the same word, 'stapled'. In round two we doubled our scores with different words constructed from the same seven letters: I made 'caution', while Sam came up with 'auction'. It seemed likely that we could have done better, which proved to be the case. Not only could we have had 'curation' for eight: a nine-letter word had gone undetected. When Susie uttered the word 'incubator', I couldn't believe my ears! As I mentioned earlier, it was a word that Sue had given me as a practice conundrum, and I had already spent some time grappling with this very set of letters!

I put my disappointment to one side and got on with the game: in round three I took the lead when my 'unloads' beat Sam's 'hounds'. From Sam's next selection the eight-letter word 'practice' stood out. Sam had revealed that she was a keyboardist, while I am a flautist, so it seemed quite appropriate that we both noticed this word. Sam was first to declare that she had spotted an eight. When I followed suit, Richard commented: 'Oh, come on you beast!' He was starting to call me that quite regularly now.

It was my turn to select the numbers. Aware that I was facing another serious challenge, I opted for 'four from the top', aiming to play to my strengths. A target of 670 proved beyond us, although we claimed seven points apiece with 673. Carol managed to produce a solution before the interval. Watching this show again for the purposes of writing this book, I realised how much I had improved in the interim period. A solution that entailed making 67 from the four large numbers and multiplying by the two small numbers (5 and 2) came to me instantly. It reinforced my belief that perseverance and practice are the keys to developing your prowess at Countdown.

A seven-point advantage at the end of the first 'half' became a thirteen-point lead at the end of round six: my 'lowers' was sufficient to beat Sam's 'worms'. Susie could find nothing better.

Another difficult selection limited us to six points apiece in the ensuing letters game. 'Gauzes' was the best anyone could do. In round eight I deliberated for some seconds over the legitimacy of the word 'retile'. When the time came to declare I decided against risking it, even though Sam had already said that she was going to try a 'seven'. It turned out that we had both made errors of judgement. Sam's dodgy agent noun, *'exalter'* wasn't listed, enabling me to add six points to my score with 'retail'. And when Susie checked 'retile' it transpired that this was in fact a valid word.

Neither of us spotted the eight-letter word, 'literate'. Jeremy Beadle pointed this out, but made it clear that the credit for noticing it belonged to Susie.

My lead was now nineteen points - not a margin I considered to be safe. There was stalemate in the last letters game of that 'half': Sam and I scored six points apiece with 'peanut' and 'planet' respectively. An easy target of 376 resulted from Sam's first choice of numbers, and our scores moved on to 70:51 with one 'half' remaining.

Round eleven produced another awkward selection, and for most of the thirty seconds I couldn't get beyond a five. In the nick of time I spotted 'sonata'. This was enough to extend my lead, as Sam had got stuck on 'stand'. I felt for her at this point: I knew she must have been kicking herself for missing a musical term.

Another last-moment spot secured eight points for me in the next letters game. I was still satisfying myself that all the letters required for 'dumbness' were there, and that it was definitely a word, when Richard asked for my declaration. Sam had seen the seven-letter word which, until the last moment, I had been expecting to submit: 'subside'. Susie commented that to get to an eight was 'impressive' - this was praise indeed, coming from someone so knowledgeable!

My lead was now 33 points and I was almost home and dry. I managed a seven with 'charges', which Sam matched with 'cashier'. A share of the points was sufficient to ensure a fourth victory for me. I was halfway to becoming an octochamp.

In the penultimate round, Sam became the first person to beat me at a numbers game, when I failed to find a means of calculating 818. Sam made it look all too easy. At this point I realised that it had become a habit of mine to carry on looking towards the board even after Carol had finished putting the numbers up, rather than focusing on the monitor, or on the sheet of paper on which I had written the numbers. With hindsight, I feel sure that I was putting myself at a disadvantage by doing this, perhaps because it was more difficult to shut out the distracting background noises and movements within the studio. It was the third time in four shows that I had missed a relatively straightforward target and it was beginning to dawn on me that I wasn't performing to my usual standard in the numbers games.

The scores stood at 91:60. I could still notch up a third successive century by getting the conundrum.

Richard pressed the button and GUTPURRIN appeared on the monitor. The ending stood out, but the presence of two 'u's among the remaining letters was perplexing at first. I persisted, and after about five seconds 'rupturing' fell into place. An excited Richard proclaimed a *fifth* victory for me: I put him straight with a smile.

After the show we said goodbye to Sam, who, unlike the other contestants, was not stopping in the hotel that night. Sam asked me for my autograph, which was very flattering! My next opponent was John Crockett, who was in charge of the guardroom at RAF Coningsby. John was cheerful, and seemed quite confident: I had heard him observe that I could be beaten at the numbers games.

The recording began at around 8pm. We had been at the studio for several hours now, but I wasn't finding it mentally tiring. For me, the main effects of the experience seemed to be physical: a loss of appetite, and an increased need to answer the call of nature!

Damian Eadie had mentioned at the start of the day that apart from the octochamps, of whom there had now been six so far in the series, the best performances involved five wins and four wins. With only about a dozen shows remaining to be filmed before the quarter-finals, I knew that one more win would put me in a very strong position to make it to the closing stages of the series. I felt determined to be at my best and give myself every opportunity of success.

Before the show Jeremy Beadle, who was to be in Dictionary Corner for the last time, said to me that he wanted to give my novel an extra plug, and that he had an idea about how to do it. I was very grateful for this suggestion. It turned out that he had come up with his own view of what 'A Nightmare in *Paradise*' might involve - spending some time on a desert island in the Maldives with . . . Jeremy Beadle!

It was time to find out whether I could end the day undefeated. The contest began with a tied letters game: the eight-letter word 'jealousy' somehow seemed to stand out. John and I both came out with 'shouted' in round two, but there was a longer word which we missed: 'hideouts'. In round three I managed an eight, which I had seen towards the end of the thirty seconds: 'armoured'. This surpassed John's 'remould' to give me the lead. In round four the points were shared with 'smelted'.

Mindful of John's comment that I might be vulnerable on the numbers, I opted for 'one from the top, and five small numbers', hoping for an easy target and the chance to take a decisive advantage during the course of the remaining letters games: a target of 104 proved so straightforward that John was able to arrive at it by adding some of the small numbers to the 75! At the first interval I led by 40 points to 32.

We resumed with a difficult letters selection, from which John produced 'chrome', while I had 'heroic'. There was another stalemate in round seven, in which John matched my 'platers' with 'palates'. At this point I was fully expecting this game to be close. At last in round eight I managed to extend my lead: I came up with the seven-letter word 'rooting'. John would have equalled this with 'rooking', had he not declared it as being a 'six'! It may be that this mistake unsettled John, because he proceeded to miss several possible seven-letter words in the next round, declaring a six in the form of 'facile'. I spotted 'reclaim', and suddenly I was 22 points ahead.

Predictably, John went for a difficult numbers game option: 'six small ones'. I was fortunate to see a way of arriving at the target of 485 fairly early in the thirty seconds. John found an alternative method, and the scores moved on to 77:55 with five rounds remaining.

During the interval I had a light-hearted chat with John about karaoke. I had discovered when Richard had introduced him that it was a hobby we shared.

I was five minutes away from being certain that I would be coming back the next day. By now my mind was really motoring, and I didn't feel at all nervous. However, I was aware there was no room for complacency.

Round eleven produced a difficult letters selection, from which we both came up with 'bonnet'. The word 'tarries' stood out in round twelve; John saw this too. I just needed one more tied round to make the game safe. In round thirteen

I spotted the seven-letter word 'candles', and felt fairly sure there was nothing better. When John declared a seven, too, I knew I couldn't lose. John also came up with 'candles', prompting Richard to reminisce about the famous sketch in which Ronnie Barker attempted to buy 'fork handles' - misunderstood as 'four candles' by shopkeeper Ronnie Corbett.

I was poised to make a fourth successive century. But John hadn't finished with the testing numbers games. He asked for 'three from the top, and three small numbers'. A target of 927 didn't immediately look achievable. 925 could be found easily enough: $(2 \times 50 \times 9) = 900$, plus $25 = 925$. I was still making the mistake of looking over towards the numbers board instead of concentrating on the monitor. I remember getting the impression that 927 seemed to be eluding Carol as well. Suddenly it occurred to me that 927 was a multiple of 9. From there it was a short step to calculating that I could make the necessary 103 by adding $(75/25)$ to (2×50).

It was the first time that I had come up with a solution to a numbers game that gave me a real sense of satisfaction. 'Here's the beast!' remarked Richard when I declared 927, as compared with John's 925. 'Oh, very good!' said Carol when she realised where my calculations were leading.

It only remained to see whether I could keep alive my 100% record with the conundrums, and in so doing beat my previous best score of 111 in the game against Ronnie. When LIBRALINT appeared on the monitor I pressed the buzzer straight away: I felt sufficiently confident that it was 'brilliant' that I didn't give myself any chance to check it.

Richard prompted the audience to repeat the word 'brilliant' as a way of passing comment on my performance. The final score was 117:75. I had taken maximum points in thirteen rounds, and it was the first time I had scored points in every round of a contest.

We were soon back at the hotel. The first moment Sue and I had in private was in the lift on the way up to our room. The moment the lift door shut behind us Sue gave me an enormous hug, and exclaimed: 'You've done it! You've made your name!' It was a moment to cherish. Sue knew how much I wanted to be taken seriously as a writer. Time would tell how much difference the day's events would make in that respect.

A celebratory drink in the hotel bar was a must. Of the contestants who had shared the Countdown experience with us, the majority were staying the night. Brian had gone, but John and his wife Bev, Ronnie and Margaret all joined us in the bar. There was a football match taking place that evening, involving the Scottish national side. The television was on in the bar, and Ronnie was listening out for the score. When it came to light that Scotland were losing, I went to commiserate with him. 'Don't worry,' Ronnie replied. 'I've got money on the other side!'

After a couple of drinks we said goodnight to the others, before heading for bed. Margaret, who was leaving early the next day, asked us to let her know whether I went on to become an octochamp. At this point I still hadn't recovered my appetite. It was only after it had become too late at night to do anything about it that I started to feel hungry. This, together with the lingering feelings of excitement about the day's events, meant that I struggled to get to sleep, and soon developed a headache which I couldn't shake off. Despite an early night, I only managed about two hours' sleep. Sue didn't sleep well either. It didn't augur well for the following day's encounters!

Chapter 5: A zombie on the set!

I had worked out that, to be sure of a place in the quarter-finals, I had to win the first game of the day. This would guarantee a further appearance on the show, and the points accumulated from these two games would be sufficient to ensure that I moved into seventh place in the list of top-scoring competitors. However, if I lost the first game, I might have only enough points to move into eighth place – thereby filling the last slot in the line-up for the quarter-finals. With around a dozen episodes remaining before the climax of the series, there would still be an opportunity for someone to overtake me. By contrast, seventh place would leave me safe, as there weren't enough shows left for two people to run up the points totals required to knock me out of the top eight.

Moreover, my average score on the first day suggested that if I won three more games it would be a close call as to whether I could overtake Paul Gallen's points total to become number one seed. There was everything to play for; yet I arrived at the studio that morning feeling like a zombie!

We soon learned that Countdown had been given a 'conundrum' by one of the day's contestants. Lisa explained the situation: Charlotte had checked on a non-arrival, only to discover that the person concerned had mistaken the date of their appearance. That day's reserve player had already been called upon to appear, in anticipation of the contingency that, were I to go on to win eight games, two fresh contestants would be required for the fourth show of the day. So Charlotte set about tracking down someone else who would be willing and able to fill the gap at very short notice. Happily, she was able to save the day by arriving at a solution within the time available!

My opponent for the first game of the day was Alan Gordon, another Scotsman. In Dictionary Corner for the first time - much to the delight of the ladies in the audience - was the Irish heartthrob singer Daniel O'Donnell. Like Jeremy before him, Daniel was very friendly and easy to talk to. He turned out to have a formidable sense of humour too.

Once Richard had finished the introductions, it fell to me to get the game under way. My first choice of letters yielded an unpromising lot: nobody, including Susie, managed more than a five-letter word. An indication of how below par I was can be found in the fact that I declared a risky word, 'loons' (which proved to be acceptable), having missed the obvious one spotted by Alan: 'boils'.

Round two saw the first of a number of oversights: there were various sevens, of which 'drastic' was the least esoteric word. I managed a six with 'racist', and was fortunate that Alan could only match it with 'gratis'. This left me in a position from where I was able to take the lead in round three, risking 'pounder' to beat Alan's five-letter word 'upend'. Another seven ('minuted') in round four was sufficient to double my lead, after Alan had got stuck on 'quiet'.

In the hope of an easy numbers game I opted for one large number and five small ones, telling Carol I had decided to be kind to her! A target of 707 proved tricky, as there were no 7s among the small numbers. I managed two below, while

Alan was two above. Carol had managed to get slightly closer with 706. I led by 32 points to 18 at the end of the first 'half'.

Daniel O'Donnell filled the entertainment spot by telling a genuinely funny tall story. After the break I thought I had built on my lead when Alan declared a six ('forces') to my seven. However, it turned out that there was no such word as '*refects*', although Susie did say that there probably had been such a word at some time in the past! The gap closed to eight points, and it stayed that way after round seven: I saw 'routing', while Alan had 'touring'. Susie pointed out that we could have had an eight-letter word: 'gyration'.

Another symptom of my fatigue made itself apparent in round eight: I identified the eight-letter word 'porridge', but couldn't convince myself I had spelt it correctly! When Richard asked me for my declaration, my uncertainty was obvious. 'How do you spell porridge?' I stammered when Richard enquired as to what was puzzling me. 'Well, how *do* you spell porridge?' he replied. As I called out the letters, I realised that I had spelt it properly. 'It just didn't look right,' I explained, feeling somewhat embarrassed. As Alan had declared a six ('griped'), I was able to extend my lead to sixteen points. The gap increased to twenty-three points in round nine, when my 'fertile' beat Alan's 'smiler'.

A difficult numbers game followed. 977 proved too much to ask, although Carol eventually came up with a solution during the break. My 975 proved good enough to add seven points to my advantage.

In round eleven, as I was selecting the letters I noticed the potential for the word 'matador'. Indeed, the first seven letters on the board were those required for this word.

However, I somehow failed to spot this, and was stuck on a six-letter word: 'roamed'. Alan did spot 'matador' enabling him to close the gap to 23 points. I still wasn't quite home and dry in this game. We both managed 'ambush' from an awkward selection in round twelve, although Susie had gone one better with 'mousaka'.

At last in round thirteen I was able to take an unassailable lead through the eight-letter word 'pulsated', outdoing Alan's 'pleated'. I took maximum points from the final numbers game, using the 10 to good effect in obtaining a target of 434. As Alan had managed 435, I moved 41 points ahead.

The conundrum took some working out, but I managed to turn DEEPSTUDI into 'deputised' after about sixteen seconds. This took the final scores onto 95:44, which seemed an unfair reflection of our respective merits. When Richard asked Alan how long he had waited to appear on Countdown, Alan replied that it was 'about twenty-two years'. When I heard that, I felt sorry for him, especially as some of the audience laughed at this answer.

I could now be certain of a place in the quarter-finals. But a winning score of less than one hundred meant that I had slipped behind schedule in my quest to become number one seed. I would now need to average around 110 in the last two games if I were to overtake Paul Gallen's total.

In the 'hot seat' during the game against Alan was Keith Jones, a tube driver who worked on the Central Line. I had chatted to Keith earlier in the day, and had formed the impression that he was a very intelligent person who would be a serious challenger. It transpired that Keith had spotted 'deputised'. When asked how he felt about taking part in the next game, he replied that he was 'a bit nervous'. His body language seemed to reinforce this remark.

The recording session had begun earlier than on the previous day. It was the last of three consecutive days' filming, and the schedule was designed to allow those who were travelling home afterwards to have a relatively early finish. My contest against Keith was to be followed by a lunch break. I was still feeling groggy, and was looking forward to some nourishment.

Keith's nervousness was reflected in his poor start to the game. In round one he came up with 'pirate'. I was then asked for my seven-letter word. I stated rather apologetically that I had 'pirated'. Another 'seven' ('boasted') was sufficient to win round two for me, after Keith came up with an unacceptable word: '*obiate*s'. Susie drew our attention to 'bastide' (a palace); Carol promptly claiming an eight by adding a leftover 's'. I moved further ahead in round three, after Keith had got stuck on a five ('route'), whereas I saw 'retook'. Poor Keith was yet to score; however he put that right in round four, declaring 'traffic' to surpass my six-letter word 'fiacre'. Susie dazzled us all with the eight-lettered 'artifice'.

Despite the fact that I had carried on making the same mistake I had made the previous day of looking across at the numbers board, I managed to come up with 557 in the first numbers game, to extend my lead to 30:7 at the first interval. This was preceded by another tall story from Daniel O'Donnell; like the one he had told earlier in the day, this had an ecclesiastical theme.

The most satisfying moment of this contest followed in round six. Keith had almost finished selecting the letters, when I noticed that if an 'r' came up the eight-letter word 'exordial' would be there. Keith opted for a final consonant, and an 'r' did indeed appear! I had the luxury of spending the whole thirty seconds looking for a nine, which seemed highly unlikely to be there, given that the leftover letter was a 'g'. Richard was gushing with praise for my word, but in reality it was just lucky that it happened to be in the forefront of my mind. It had featured on a show televised a few weeks before: the selection concerned had also yielded 'uxorial' (wifely), which I had spotted (along with that day's champion, Robert Harris). I remember feeling confident that 'uxorial' would be the best word available, until Susie revealed 'exordial' (relating to an exordium, the introduction to a treatise), of which I had never heard.

It took the scores on to 38:7. I appeared to be running away with it! Keith moved into double figures in the next round with 'washed', which I matched with 'showed'.

In round eight I was faced with a moral dilemma. I had seen the six-letter word 'molten'. I was looking at using the word 'moon' as a prefix or suffix in combination with some of the other letters, when I overheard Susie whisper 'moonlet' to Daniel. It was a word I knew, but I couldn't be sure I would have seen it. So I assumed that I wouldn't have done so, and declared 'molten'. Keith also declared a six, but his word '*mentol*' was disallowed. This was the only time in any show in which I was involved that I became aware of anything that was said in Dictionary Corner, as Susie and the celebrities were always very discreet.

With a lead of 50 points to 13 I seemed certain to be on my way to a seventh successive win. But Keith was just getting going! In the next round he came up with 'consular' for eight points. This time it was my turn to have a word disallowed, albeit only a seven. I knew that 'blanco' could be a verb, so tried '*blancos*'; however, the third person singular in the present tense is, in fact, 'blancoes'. Susie remarked that Keith's word was 'fantastic', prompting Richard to comment that this was becoming her favourite compliment.

Keith made further inroads into the deficit by taking ten points in the numbers game which followed, coming up with a canny way of creating 595 while I could only manage 593.

At the end of the second part of the show my lead had been reduced to 19 points. Remarkably, there had been only one round in which we had both added points to our totals. However, there was another tied round at the start of the third 'half' of the contest, when Keith came up with 'mounted', while I saw 'minuted' for the second successive show.

An awkward looking selection followed. The best I could manage was 'gamma', of which I was uncertain. When Keith declared that he had a dodgy six, I made up my mind not to risk 'gamma' and to settle for the safe four-letter word 'game'. When Keith came out with '*gammel*' I felt confident that I would be able to extend my lead beyond twenty points. Richard asked him what he thought it meant. 'I don't know, I just need the points!' was Keith's reply.

Susie checked the dictionary and confirmed that there was no such word as '*gammel*'. The scores moved on to 61:38. A share of the points in the final letters game would ensure victory for me. STREAILER looked like a particularly promising selection. However, I struggled to get past the seven-letter word 'retails'. Late on in the thirty seconds I spotted one better: 'trailers'. I would be home and dry as long as Keith didn't have a nine - but I had a sneaking feeling that there was a nine somewhere in the combination! Sitting in the audience, Sue had seen that it was possible to get 'retailers', and was disappointed when I only declared an eight. I was lucky: Keith had also got stuck on 'trailers', and the game was safe.

I extended my advantage with ten points in the final numbers game, finding the target of 636 by adding some small numbers to the 50 to get 63, multiplying by 10, and adding the 6. Could I finish the game with a flourish by solving the conundrum? EATRHCLAD appeared on the screen. I experimented with the suffix '-head', but couldn't see anything to put with it. Nor could I produce a word ending in '-ed' or '-ated'. I kept trying to the bitter end, but remained as clueless as I had been at the start of the thirty seconds. It was really disappointing to hear the whole of the theme tune for the first time in the final round of a contest.

When Richard revealed that the answer was in fact 'cathedral', I felt somewhat reassured, because at least it wasn't an obvious word. It would have been more irritating to miss a word with one of the regular endings. Nevertheless, every time I see a delivery lorry with the logo for the firm 'Cathedral' on the side I am reminded of this moment!

It rounded off a rather lack-lustre performance. I had managed the maximum score in just seven rounds, and had failed to score in four of the others. My final total was 79, to Keith's 46. It effectively put an end to my chance of becoming number one seed. It meant that the main objective of my eighth game was to become an octochamp. From the 'hot seat', my opponent for the last game, Diane Crews, joked that she should catch a train home now.

At lunchtime Sue advised me to make sure I had plenty of nourishment. My appetite seemed to have returned, and after I tucked into a salad I felt refreshed and ready for action.

Before the game Daniel O'Donnell, sensing that Diane wasn't relishing the prospect, said to me: 'You don't mind if you lose this one, do you?' Even as I said 'no', I thought that in reality the answer was 'yes'! I wanted to join the ranks of the octochamps. In his introduction to the show Richard acknowledged that I was on the verge of achieving this. He congratulated me on some 'great performances', and said that I was a 'charming gentleman to boot'.

I began the game by missing a word that I should have seen. I had 'outrage' for seven, which Diane saw too. Daniel drew our attention to the fact that we could have inserted an 'n' to make the eight-letter word 'outrange', a word which has often featured on the show over the years.

Diane's first choice of letters yielded such a bizarre lot that it was difficult to spot anything at all. I was relieved to notice the five-letter word 'oasis' some way into the thirty seconds, without which I would have been struggling to get more than a two! Diane guessed at '*suis*', which wouldn't have been allowed. She was unlucky in round three when Susie checked '*tabler*' and found it to be absent from the dictionary. I took six points with 'tribal', but I missed some sevens, in the form of 'librate' and 'tablier'. Watching the show again at a later date, I realised that we all missed the eight letter-word 'pubertal'.

I went further ahead in the next round, finding 'maltose' from among a selection of sevens, to beat Diane's 'medals'. In the first numbers game I found the target of 437 relatively easily. When Diane missed out with 438, Richard remarked: 'He's a bit like that, you know!' By the end of the first 'half' I had opened up a 28-point lead.

After the interval Diane boldly went for an eight, but *'pyrenean'* was disallowed. I didn't feel entirely confident of 'pannier' (a basket), but Susie confirmed I had spelt it correctly. Another ropy selection then yielded fives apiece: I had 'flick', while Diane had 'flock'. Round eight was also tied: Diane came up with 'worsted', which I matched with 'towered'. Susie introduced us to 'wormseed' (a plant).

I was ahead by 54 points to 19. After Diane had declared a six ('bilges') to my seven in the next round, Richard asked me what I had seen. 'Visible,' I replied, with a smile: I knew it was inevitable that Richard would chuckle about the fact that I had seen visible!

Diane asked for a 'Whitehall' selection of numbers: one from the top row, two from the next, then one from the row below, and two from the bottom row (after Whitehall 1212 - the old phone number for Scotland Yard). This option results in one large number and five small ones. A target of 977 looked tricky, but we managed to find alternative ways of arriving at it. When Diane gave her explanation, she rounded it off by subtracting a couple of small numbers which she had actually intended to add. Happily Carol knew what Diane was trying to do and put her straight. It was typical of the fairness and supportiveness that the Countdown team show towards all of the contestants.

At the interval I led by 71 points to 29. Barring something remarkable, I was going to achieve my objective. I wanted to savour the moment. However, I was feeling uncomfortable, as I needed (not for the first time while on the set) to answer the call of nature. So I asked for time to attend to this during the second interval. I had prepared myself mentally and emotionally for the experience of taking part in Countdown. I hadn't anticipated that it would have such an effect on my metabolism!

When I returned I still had a little work to do to make sure of victory. Diane was unfortunate in round eleven, declaring a six when she actually had a seven, in the shape of 'trodden'. My 'donated' was sufficient to win the round. But there were better words on offer: 'ratooned' (from 'ratoon', to crop plants so that they grow new shoots) and 'deodorant'. I had missed another nine-letter word, albeit a difficult one to spot.

I was keeping a close eye on the score now, watching out for the moment when it would become mathematically impossible for Diane to catch me and my 'octavianship' would be confirmed. I worked out that I just needed a share of the points in round twelve. When Diane declared a six ('mascot'), I declined the seven-letter word 'somatic', of which I wasn't entirely certain, in favour of a safe six, in the form of 'stigma'.

And so I was in the enviable position of being able to celebrate an eighth successive win with three rounds to spare. Anyone who noticed the breadth of my smile at this moment might have wondered what I was grinning at! My last choice of letters yielded the eight-letter word 'profiler', which won the round at the expense of Diane's 'parole'.

Daniel expressed his admiration, saying that it was 'the last word to Mark'.

Diane's final selection was 'an inverted T', another combination which produces one large number and five small ones. 538 eluded everybody. Diane and I shared the points with 535; Carol edged closer with 540.

I had moved on to 99 points, with just the conundrum remaining. LILAQGUNS suggested the word 'squalling' straight away, but I wasn't convinced that 'squall' could be a verb, as well as a noun, so I spent a couple of seconds trying to see whether I could find an alternative solution. Even when I pressed the buzzer I still wasn't sure. Richard commented on my uncertainty, before confirming that I had secured the ten points I required to amass a fifth century. The final score was 109:42. It was my largest winning margin, and I had managed to score in every round for the second time. Although I had achieved the maximum score in only eight rounds, it was certainly an improvement on my performance in the game against Keith. This was at least partly attributable to the fact that the feeling of fatigue which had hindered me during the morning was wearing off.

In his résumé of my run on the show, Richard affirmed that I was the seventh octavian of the series. It was only as he said this that the magnitude of the challenge I now faced really struck home to me. I was looking at Richard with a rather rueful expression when he added:

'Of all the octavians, you're pretty good, you're the number three seed'.

I already knew that I wouldn't have accumulated enough points to overtake either Paul Gallen or Jack Welsby, so it was consoling to know that I was at least ahead of the two octavians whose shows were yet to be screened.

In saying farewell to Diane, Richard remarked that she was 'up against greatness', which made me feel very proud - Richard had witnessed every performance in the history of Countdown. He added: 'He might be the eventual winner, you never know.' Diane replied with good humour: 'Well, I can say I played against him, can't I?'

After the show there was another photo-shoot for the contestants who had taken part in that day's filming. Richard seemed to think they were trying to cram too many people in. It occurred to me that perhaps I wasn't supposed to be in it, having been part of the previous day's line-up! But Carol dismissed Richard's comments, and assured me that I was supposed to be there.

Two shows remained to be filmed that day. Although we had a long journey home ahead of us, Sue and I decided to remain for the first of these, so that we could have the experience of being in the studio audience together. An extra treat was in store for those who were in the studio before the start of this show. Prior to taking his seat on the set, Daniel O'Donnell had come to have a chat with the audience. He readily agreed to sing, despite the fact that he would have to do so unaccompanied. There was a complete hush as he delivered a traditional Irish lullaby in a soft voice, effortlessly bringing tears to the eyes of the some of the ladies in the audience!

I soon discovered that the overwhelming majority of the audience had come equipped with pen and paper, to play along with the contestants on the set! Ironically, at this point I was trying *not* to do that, but to enjoy viewing the show from a different perspective. When you're in the studio audience, the monitor showing the letters and numbers boards is located overhead. This makes it more difficult to play along, as you have to crane your neck, which isn't conducive to concentration.

We watched an intriguing contest between Judith Armstrong and Brian Lightfoot, which the former won on a crucial conundrum. The fact that we had met the contestants briefly in the Green Room (during which time I had given them encouragement and reassurance that the experience wouldn't be nerve-wracking) added to the appeal of watching them take part in the show. After that we felt compelled to stay for the last game of the day, in which Judith saw off the challenge of Alex Lacy. It crossed my mind that there were enough shows left in series 52 for Judith to extend her winning run long enough to secure a place in the quarter-finals. It turned out that she didn't quite make it - although at the end of her last show she implied that this was something of a relief!!

The last minutes of our first visit to the studio were spent with Diane and her husband. They took the outcome of my match with Diane very well, and we chatted amicably as we made our way back to the hotel.

Sue and I were soon on our way back to London. We were both really excited about the way things had turned out. Sue described the experience as a visit to 'Planet Countdown', because, she said, it was like entering another world, where everything is fun and everyone is friendly. What's more, we knew we would be going back just a few weeks later. With typical efficiency, Countdown had advised all contestants in advance of the recording dates, in case they were called upon to participate: the quarter-finals would be filmed on Tuesday 9th and Wednesday 10th November. It was now Thursday 14th October. I had less than four weeks in which to prepare for the challenge!

Chapter 6: Back to work

Sue had found that it soothed her nerves during my games to record details of the selections, targets, declarations and scores. I looked back through the sheets of paper she had used to see what I had missed. Most disappointing was the fact that I had failed to spot four of the five nine-letter words. If I had seen all five I would have garnered another 50 points. That would have been sufficient for me to become number one seed. As it was, my total was 811, 35 behind Paul Gallen and 20 behind Jack Welsby.

I felt that I needed to improve quite substantially if I were to have a real chance of becoming overall champion of the series. So I practised hard during the few weeks leading up to the quarter-finals, focusing particularly on nine-letter words. I was becoming convinced of the effectiveness of the technique I had devised of using squares of paper with the letters in a grid on one side and the words they formed on the other. The one nine-letter word that I had spotted ('printhead') was on one of them. So I set about compiling more of these squares, which I carried with me in my pocket, taking every opportunity to peruse them. For instance, I would take them out of my pocket whenever I was waiting in a queue. By the time we returned to 'Planet Countdown', I must have had well over a thousand such squares, each containing between four and six words. Building such a collection had been a laborious, time-consuming process, but one that I hoped would prove profitable.

As soon as we returned from Leeds, people wanted to know how I had got on. I demurred as far as possible, because I wanted them to have the excitement of seeing the games in which I was involved as though they were live and the outcome uncertain. My parents and family had insisted on being updated as things happened, and Sue had taken care of this through regular texts and calls from her mobile. I had to tell my colleagues how I had fared, because I needed to ensure that I would be granted the leave to return for the quarter-finals. Otherwise, unless people insisted that they would rather know, I kept them in the dark. The vast majority of my friends had no idea what to expect when they first watched my shows. The one thing I needed to tell people was that the transmission date of my début on Countdown was a day earlier than I had originally told them, because of the rescheduling that occurred on the first day.

The programmes to be transmitted during the period leading up to the quarter-finals would feature the two remaining octochamps. I got my first glimpse of one of them, John Hunt, in the episodes we had set the VCR to record while we were at Leeds.

I remembered that while we were at the studios Carol had voiced her admiration for John's prowess at the numbers games, and it was soon obvious why. John consistently opted for 'six small numbers', and unfailingly delivered solutions which reflected his expertise. He was only marginally less impressive at the word games. Although my record when 'playing along' with his performances was good (I would have won six out of eight), there was one game which stood out in my mind as a real wake-up call. John saw the nine-letter word 'corpulent', at a time when he would already have been ahead of me, opening up a gap which would ultimately have amounted to around 40 points. I couldn't remember the last time I would have lost so heavily!

Shortly after John's run had come to an end, there was a game between the two contestants who were to complete the line-up for the quarter-finals: Rita Wilmott and Steve Moir. Rita seemed to surprise herself with her success, stringing together a sequence of five wins. Anyone watching without foreknowledge of what Steve Moir was to achieve would have been convinced that it would become six when Rita opened up a healthy lead over the Scot. But Steve completed a remarkable recovery by seeing the conundrum in a fraction of a second to snatch victory. The sequence of games which led to his becoming the sixth octochamp of series 52 was still in progress when the time came for us to return to Leeds.

Chapter 7: Return to 'Planet Countdown'

Immediately before the quarter-finals I derived inspiration from a sporting heroine of mine. On the afternoon of Sunday November 7th Sue and I were about to embark on the first leg of the journey to 'Planet Countdown' - from my flat in Hove to Sue's home in London. Just as we were ready to leave I remembered that the New York Marathon was taking place, and that Paula Radcliffe was taking part. It was her comeback race, following the Athens Olympics in which she had come to a stop in both the marathon and the 10,000 metres. I didn't expect that Paula would be back to her best, and would not have been surprised to learn that she was out of contention. However, when I switched on the television to check on her progress, it turned out that she was in the midst of a titanic struggle with Kenya's Susan Chepkemei. The contest was so compelling that we kept postponing our journey until it became clear who was going to prevail. This didn't happen until the very end of the race, when Paula drove hard for the line, to see off her opponent by just four seconds. Her triumph served as a reminder that things do sometimes go better than expected, and that determination and perseverance can pay dividends. Although we had made our return to London later than expected, from the point of view of raising our spirits it was well worth the delay!

On the evening of Monday 8th November we completed the journey to Leeds. Sue was working during the daytime, whereas I had taken the day off to complete my preparations. Just before we left I played along with the latest in Steve Moir's run of games. The outcome would have been a tie, which was disappointing given that I had 'won' the previous games in which Steve was involved. I knew that I couldn't feel entirely confident of beating any of the other octavians.

By this time I knew who my quarter-final opponent was going to be. It was to be sixth seed John Gray, who would become the third Scot I had faced (following Margaret Boyle and Ronnie Boyd). While watching John's run of success I had admired his composure and unassuming nature, not to mention his obviously personable character, and felt that ours would be a game played in the best spirit. Whoever came out on top would face the winner of the contest between second seed Jack Welsby and seventh seed David Thirlwall. In the other half of the draw top seed Paul Gallen was to compete against Rita Wilmott, the only female player to have made the quarter-finals, and the only participant who wasn't defending an unbeaten record. Completing the line-up was the match between John Hunt and Steve Moir, who had ended up fourth and fifth seeds respectively.

I was aware that I had one slight advantage over everyone else: I had seen all of them compete, whereas none of them had seen me before, as my games were yet to be screened.

We arrived at the hotel in Leeds after midnight. There was no cause for concern about the lack of an early night. We weren't due at the studio until just after midday on the Tuesday, and, although all the quarter-finalists had been asked to attend that day's recording, the schedule ensured that I wasn't due to compete until the first show on Wednesday morning.

At breakfast time we saw some of those we recognised from television 'in the flesh' for the first time. Paul Gallen was there, with a gentleman who we assumed was his father. We also spotted John Hunt, looking relaxed as he read his newspaper. I decided to remain incognito until we got to the studio. There would be plenty of time for making the others' acquaintance after that.

Sue and I made our way to the studio in good time, and were among the first to arrive. We were both excited to be back, although Sue's high hopes were mixed with apprehension.

Gradually all the contestants gathered in the reception area. As well as the eight seeded players, Robert Harris, who had won four games, had been asked to appear as a standby. However, everyone arrived as expected, so unluckily Robert didn't get to take part. Among the last people we met were my quarter-final opponent John Gray and his wife Jo. We struck up a good rapport with them, regardless of the fact that John and I were rivals for the Countdown crown. They had a great sense of humour and were very pleasant company.

The first three games of the day were not part of the quarter-finals, but were those bringing series 52 to a close. In the Green Room, the atmosphere among those of us who were watching these games while waiting to take part in the knockout stages was at first cagey. Nobody seemed to want to reveal what they were thinking, or appear to be trying to outdo the others. Steve Moir was the person who was most ready to change this. The affable Scot was naturally communicative. When the fourth game of the day - the first quarter-final between Paul Gallen and Rita Wilmott - began, most of the other contenders opted to take a seat in the studio audience. However, Steve and I remained in the Green Room. Encouraged by Steve's openness, I relaxed my guard, and the two of us exchanged observations freely. The opening contest was not a classic. Paul was always ahead of Rita, and having spotted the nine-letter word 'transomed' went on to win quite comfortably.

The final show to be recorded that day was the second quarter-final, between Jack Welsby and David Thirlwall. In anticipation of our match the following morning, it fell to John Gray and me to take our places in the 'hot seats'. As this involved sitting right at the front of the audience, the monitors above us were at a steeper angle than they had been when Sue and I sat at the rear of the audience during our previous visit. Although I had decided not to try to compete with Jack and David, I was nevertheless curious to see what would spring to mind effortlessly. Halfway through the game John whispered to me that he had seen a nine ('menstrual'), which had escaped my notice, as well as that of the two contestants on the set. What's more, when the conundrum came along, I was unable to solve it. Jack, who was well ahead in the game, and David were also stumped. When Richard asked whether anyone in the audience had the solution, the only hand that went up belonged to John, who revealed that the answer was 'nauseated'. John then amused the audience by expressing his concern that he might have peaked too soon. Richard noted that I hadn't spotted the conundrum, and asked how I would have fared in the game.

'Other than that it was all right,' I affirmed with an exaggerated note of confidence. In reality I knew that I would have needed to overcome a deficit of twenty-eight points over thirteen rounds had I been playing against John in this game. The experience in the 'hot seat' was hardly a confidence booster! But I remained optimistic: it was unlikely that anything comparable would occur the next day.

Sue had been sitting with John's wife Jo close behind, though not directly behind, the 'hot seats'. As the cameras focused on John and me at the end of the show, Jo - knowing that Sue was camera-shy and was positioning herself behind John in order to keep out of the limelight - mischievously tried to push Sue into view of the cameras. Sue did her best to resist, and eventually kept Jo at bay, but not before she had appeared momentarily on the screen!

A quiet evening in the hotel was followed by an early night. When I awoke unusually early the next morning my mind was racing. I went through some conundrums by way of last-minute limbering up, and felt confident that I was mentally prepared for the challenge ahead. I felt equally certain that I would have to come through three tough matches if I were to realise my ambition of becoming overall series champion.

I had learned that the transmission date for the quarter-final would be 13th December - my 42nd birthday! When we had taken our places on the set, I mentioned this to Richard, who said that he would acknowledge this during the show. The set reflected the imminence of Christmas: as well as the standard decorations, there were a couple of small Countdown Christmas 'trees' - triangular boards featuring bulbs spelling out the title of the show. To blend in with the backdrop, the tree on Richard's desk was mauve, while the one in Dictionary Corner was purple. Alongside Susie was the popular comedian Richard Digance, who was making his 100th appearance on the show.

In keeping with the imaginative humour which the scriptwriters injected into the show, each of the contestants had been given a 'title' for Richard to refer to us by, during our introduction. Charlotte had tipped us off that this was going to happen, without actually telling us what our titles would be. John was described as the 'Dover Declarer', an allusion to his work as a Customs Officer, while I was introduced as the 'East Sussex Sawnoff, Mark Tournoff'!

The moment arrived for the contest to commence, and John began with a choice of letters which looked promising. Early on in the thirty seconds I identified the suffix '-ness', but having been unable to achieve an entire word containing this ending I considered other possibilities. I got as far as a seven ('softens'), before deciding to have another look for words ending in '-ness'. With a few seconds to spare I noticed the nine-letter word 'loftiness'! I knew it was definitely listed in the dictionary: it was a word I had included on one of the 'squares' I had used in practice. It turned out that John had come up with the same seven-letter word which moments before I had been expecting to declare. As a result I was able to take an eighteen-point lead at the end of the first round. It was the opposite position to the one I had been in when I had played Ronnie Boyd and he had seen 'manicured' right at the start of the game. I remember thinking that, as well as being a great way to begin the game against John, it could hardly have been a better signal to send to the remaining contestants, for whom this was to be the first indication of my prowess at Countdown! Before moving on, Richard observed that it wasn't a bad way to mark my birthday!

In round two a number of seven-letter words stood out: John opted for 'tribune', while I used the same letters to make 'turbine'. Dictionary Corner offered nothing longer. The letters in round three weren't so friendly. John came up with 'holier', while I managed 'milkier', prompting a remark that typified Richard's humour:

'Holier than thou, milkier than cow!' he enthused.

I had extended my lead to 25 points. It stayed that way at the end of round four, in which both John and I saw 'actions' for seven points. In the first numbers game 896 proved a straightforward target. At the end of the first 'half ' I led by 49 points to 24. It was a better start than I could possibly have envisaged.

Richard Digance introduced his entertainment slot by explaining that he had decided to mark his 100th appearance by rereading a poem that had provoked a great deal of interest the first time he had produced it. The poem was an amusing and highly imaginative tale of some sparrows who put on a 'Red Arrows' style air display, during which one of them flew too close to a jumbo jet and lost all his feathers.

The serious action recommenced with another tied letters game: John and I used the same seven letters to come out with 'grandee' and 'angered' respectively. However, Susie revealed that we could have gone one better with 'renegado' (a word of Spanish origin from which 'renegade' is derived). Neither of us could get beyond sixes in the next round: John produced 'pasted', while I had 'panted'. It was left to Susie to point out the sevens we could have had: 'standee' and 'pedants'.

In round eight I was able to extend my lead, having risked 'wilier', after John had come up with 'ruble'. The next selection seemed sure to contain something longer. 'Panties' was an obvious seven-letter word. However, nothing better came to mind until the very last moment, when I noticed 'pastimes', and was able to equal John's eight-letter word 'matiness' - which he had also seen too late to write down.

As I now led by 76 points to 45, I concluded that I had enough in hand to justify asking for an easy numbers selection, in the hope of notching up the sort of score that would give the rest of the opposition something to think about! So I opted for 'one large and five small numbers'. However, a target of 707 from a selection lacking in odd numbers wasn't so easy. I had to begin with 8×100 and work out how to incorporate the remaining numbers in such a way that I could produce 93 less. I managed to achieve this, whereas John was one away, enabling me to extend my advantage to 41 points. I really couldn't believe that I was that far ahead!

What happened after the second interval could easily have put a different reflection on the matter: from John's next letters selection I had quickly spotted the eight-letter word 'migrated' and was looking rather speculatively for a way of rearranging these letters to incorporate the remaining 'e' for a nine. It took about twenty seconds before it dawned on me that all I had to do was add the 'e' to the front of my existing word to make 'emigrated'. When Richard asked for our declarations, John replied that he had a nine: it turned out that he had also spotted 'emigrated'. Judging by the evidence of the video of the show, he had seen it rather earlier than I had!

When I followed John's declaration by saying that I too had a 'nine', there was a mixed reaction from the studio audience. I put this down to the fact that had John been the only one to see 'emigrated' it would have opened up the possibility of a comeback on his part and a close finish. As it was, it effectively put an end to the game as a contest between the two of us, and turned it instead into a quest for an exceptionally high score on my part. I had amassed 104 points with four rounds remaining.

My next letters selection looked a fairly promising lot. However, I struggled to get anything decent from them, eventually coming up with 'exordia' (one of the alternative plurals of 'exordium', the introduction to a treatise). It was enough to win the round, as John had got stuck on 'craned'. But I was lucky not to have been punished for failing to spot 'anorexic', which Richard Digance revealed to us.

We moved on to the final letters game, in which another seven points resulted from my seeing 'stagers'. John had already declared 'greats', prompting Richard to preface his request for me to announce my word with the remark that I was 'turning out to be one of the Countdown greats'.

My score moved on to 118. I again asked for 'one large and five small numbers', and this time was rewarded with an easy task. Both John and I arrived at 555 with time to spare.

Richard was clearly revelling in the way my score was relentlessly increasing. I had already surpassed my previous top score, and just needed the conundrum to score in every round in successive appearances.

'UNACOVERS' appeared on the monitor: immediately the word 'cavernous' sprang to mind, but I hesitated momentarily to check it before pressing the buzzer. I wanted to make sure I didn't spoil the climax of the game by getting the conundrum wrong! I needn't have been concerned. Richard unveiled the answer and the last ten points were added to my total. It took my final score up to 138, a total that I had never even approached in all the years I had been playing along at home!

Richard commiserated with John, who had been very unfortunate to finish with a total of 73 points. John graciously described my performance as 'tremendous' and added that he 'didn't mind losing to that'. I felt that the scoreline was very unrepresentative of our respective levels of competence. I knew how different a story it might have been, if we had played the previous day! And had I not produced slightly better answers on a number of occasions, John would have scored well over a century in our game.

I knew that the all-time record score for a single game, held by Julian Fell, stood at 146 points. When Richard consulted the statistics, which were obviously kept in front of him for ready reference, I was surprised to learn that my total was the second highest ever. (In fact, when I checked later, I discovered that it was identical to the second highest individual score, also attributable to Julian Fell.)

I had another pleasant surprise immediately after the show, when Richard Digance passed me the copy of the poem he had read earlier. He and Susie had both written messages on it: Richard's comment acknowledged my 42nd birthday, while Susie congratulated me on my 'star performance'.

Returning to the Green Room, I felt a great sense of satisfaction: it struck me that even if I didn't go on to win the series, I had achieved something special.

There would be a wait of several hours before I was due back on the set. There were two shows to be recorded in the meantime. First, John Hunt and Steve Moir had to contest the last of the quarter-finals. The winner would then take on Paul Gallen in the first semi-final, before Jack Welsby and I played for the other place in the final.

John and Steve had witnessed my quarter-final victory from the 'hot seats'. When Richard had asked for their comments at the end of the show, John had said that I would have been 'unbeatable' on that occasion, while Steve had said that he certainly wouldn't have done as well as I had. Their responses suggested to me that both had accepted that they were likely to come unstuck at some point.

Their match was one that I had expected to be close, and there was indeed little to choose between them during the first 'half' of the game. John took an early lead with 'croons'; however, Steve struck back with 'incline', and remained one point ahead until round six, when John spotted 'underlip'. A characteristically shrewd numbers game put John seventeen points clear at the end of the second 'half', and he extended his lead with 'manses' in round eleven. Although Steve took the points in the next round with 'detained', John was able to close out his opponent with 'hailer' in the last letters game. Steve ended his career on Countdown by spotting the conundrum 'uplighter', despite the fact that he had never come across the word before!

So it fell to John to take on the number one seed, Paul Gallen. I was back in the 'hot seat' for this show, alongside my opponent Jack. The semi-final got off to an extraordinary start. After Paul had won the first two rounds with 'locates' and 'sweatier', both contestants had *'tommies'* disallowed in round three: the entry in the dictionary is capitalised. When Paul declared a nine in round four John followed suit, but he was clearly less confident than Paul. It turned out that John had good reason to be uncertain: his *'palenoids'* was presumably a misspelling of Paul's word, namely 'palinodes' (poetical retractions). It looked as though John would finally get off the mark in the first numbers game. Having opted for his customary 'six small numbers' he declared that he had achieved the target of 383: but John had made an error in calculation and Paul was able to claim another seven points by arriving at 380.

After the interval another six points came Paul's way through 'acumen'. The score had moved on to 46:0, and John was surely beaten already. It came as a shock to me to see someone who had won all nine of his previous games being trounced in this manner. In round seven, John did get some points on the board with 'darkens', but Paul equalled this with 'asunder'. John then doubled his total with 'trefoil', but Paul matched it with 'politer', before extending his lead with 'sprained' in round nine.

After both players hit the target in the second numbers game, Paul went further ahead with 'taloned' in round eleven. Two more tied letters games followed, before Paul secured his century in the last numbers game. John was also spot on, to remain 61 points adrift. A difficult conundrum (SHINYGITE) eluded both contestants - as well as Jack and me . . . and everyone else in the studio audience! It was left to Richard to reveal that the word was in fact 'hygienist', and to congratulate Paul on an emphatic victory. The final scores were 108:47.

Chapter 8: It starts getting crucial!

With filming of the second semi-final imminent, Jack and I went to the changing room to don different shirts. Before we had finished, Paul came into the room. With just the three of us there, it occurred to me to remark: 'Well, the winner's in this room!' I felt that it was anybody's guess as to which of the three of us would ultimately prevail.

When the time came to go through to the studio, I followed Jack along the corridor, and was surprised to find that he seemed more nervous than I was. When Richard asked him how he was feeling during the preliminaries, Jack replied that he wasn't too bad, considering what he was about to take on. It seemed strange, given that I had been in awe of Jack when he first appeared on the show, to discover that he had a similar level of respect for my abilities!

As Richard was introducing me, he mentioned the fact that I was an author; he then stopped short and looked to me for a prompt. I knew exactly what he wanted, because he never could remember what my novel was called.

'A Nightmare in *Paradise,*' I said. Richard then added some comments about the copy which I had given him earlier in the day, saying that it looked an exciting read, even if it was a bit thin! (At around 55,000 words, it is shorter than the average for a novel - 70,000).

I had won the toss, which enabled me to opt for the challenger's chair, and so limit Jack to one opportunity to ask for six small numbers. It therefore fell to Jack to make the first choice of letters. It wasn't a very promising selection: nobody, including Susie, could do better than a six. I matched Jack's 'mentor' with 'remote'. We had identical seven-letter words in rounds two and three: 'paroled' was followed by 'seeding'. As the scores moved on to 20:20 Richard Digance remarked: 'It's going to be a tight one, this, isn't it?' However, the deadlock was about to be broken: in round four I could only manage 'giblets', whereas Jack saw 'librates'. It turned out to be one of several eights: Susie revealed the others to be 'tabliers' and 'regalist'.

Jack's numbers choice was to follow, and I couldn't afford to slip further behind. With a selection of numbers that were mostly at the lower end of the small-number range, 622 looked a daunting target - and so it proved. I saw 620 from a transaction that involved making 62 and multiplying this by 10. Jack came up with identical calculations, and not having written them down, had to go through them first. This meant that I needed to pass my workings to Richard so that he could verify that they were identical. I had just noticed that a 4 I had written had come out very poorly. As soon as I saw

Richard looking bemused I guessed what was puzzling him and explained what the number should be. However, Richard carried on looking perplexed, and I wondered whether he might give up on my solution and disallow it. But to my relief Richard just commented that my 4 looked more like a 1, and - after further cogitation - awarded me seven points.

The time Richard spent deliberating was actually edited from the televised version of the show, presumably because it was neither necessary nor interesting. I was quite glad about this, because I was concerned that people might have thought I didn't really have the solution I had declared.

As usual, Richard Digance provided some interesting pre-interval entertainment, describing how, during a visit to the lavatory, he had concluded that 'Gin harms a skate'. He gave the credit for this assertion to Armitage Shanks, the toilet manufacturers, whose logo had prompted him to think anagrammatically.

The contest started again with my choice of letters. From the first six letters on the board I spotted 'peanut', but could find nothing longer, even after the addition of the remaining letters. To my surprise, this was enough to reduce the deficit to 2 points, as Jack had seen nothing more than the four-letter 'feat'.

The next selection looked much more promising, and I quickly spotted the eight-letter word 'aversion'. I carried on looking to see whether there was any way of incorporating the leftover 'c', without any real expectation that I would find one. The moment when I realised that there was a nine-letter word is captured perfectly in the televised version of the show. I am shown mouthing 'Ooh!' after around twenty seconds. I quickly wrote down 'veronicas'. It was enough to win the round, seeing off Jack's 'scenario', itself an excellent spot.

In a moment which was edited from the show, Richard asked how I knew the word 'veronicas'. I assured him that it had come up in the singular fairly recently. Richard and Susie clearly had no recollection of this, but I heard a lady in the audience cry out 'Yes!' Perhaps her name was Veronica? What I didn't realise until much later was that the previous manifestation of this word had occurred, rather ironically, during one of Jack's shows. Jack must have felt pretty peeved that he had missed it a second time. 'Veronicas' was also a word that I had included on one of the practice 'squares' that I had compiled, further vindicating the use of this technique.

I suddenly found myself 16 points ahead. It was a significant advantage, but not a decisive one. In the next round, I saw the word 'mintiest' straight away, and expected that this would be sufficient to tie the round. When Jack declared that he only had a six, ('minces'), I was amazed. Now I was 24 points clear, with 7 rounds remaining. Was I really going to win comfortably?

In round nine I could manage nothing better than the five-letter word 'metal'. I wasn't hopeful that this would be enough for me to sustain my advantage. I was right: Jack had spotted a word which I didn't even recognise, 'palmate' (a botanical term), to reduce the gap to 17 points.

Any suggestion that this game was all but over had gone. But I still had enough of a lead to make a defensive numbers selection of 'one large and five small'. When a target of 998 came out I tried to work upwards from $13 \times 75 = 975$. When this proved unproductive I attempted to work downwards from $14 \times 75 = 1050$. When I was still unable to get closer than 994, I opted to experiment with multiplying by 9. I came up with a protracted way of making 111 from the remaining numbers. When I declared 999 I was optimistic that it would be sufficient for a share of the points.

'999,' Richard repeated. 'Is that an emergency for you, Jack?'

My heart sank when Jack declared that he had got 998. It turned out that he had used a method I hadn't considered, working upwards from $12 \times 75 = 900$.

With five rounds remaining, my lead had shrunk to 7 points. In the letters game which followed the interval I had the misfortune to make the most disappointing mistake of my entire 'career' on Countdown. I had written down the seven-letter word 'debited'. But I had it in mind that this word was an eight-letter word. So when I subsequently noticed that there were two letters which didn't belong in the word 'debited', I jumped to the conclusion that it wasn't possible to make this word from the selection. I could see that 'debit' was definitely there, so I crossed the '-ed' off the end and looked in vain for something longer. After I had declared 'debit' Jack almost apologetically uttered the word 'debited'. I had to admit, to my embarrassment, that I had wrongly dismissed this word. As a result the scores were level.

Carol reiterated Richard Digance's earlier observation about the closeness of the game. It served as a reminder that, although I had let a substantial lead evaporate, I was still very much in the running.

After three successive scoreless rounds, I managed to add to my total in round twelve with the seven-letter word 'resumed', which Jack matched with 'headers'. I was fortunate that he didn't see 'measured', to which Richard Digance drew our attention.

In the final letters game Jack looked set to take the lead, as he declared a six to my five. But it turned out that Jack's word '*atoner*', wasn't in the dictionary, enabling me to win the round with 'after'. We had both missed 'ornate', 'neater', and 'oftener'.

Neither of us had been involved in a close finish before. Was the pressure beginning to tell? I certainly felt less comfortable than at any previous time in my appearances on Countdown. But I was determined to take courage and to ensure that if I did go down, I would go down fighting.

Being five points ahead going into the final numbers game meant that I couldn't lose the match before the conundrum - whereas I could win it by then! I opted for 'four large numbers and two small ones'. A target of 566 looked unattainable. I managed 567, while Jack came up with 565. Carol couldn't improve on our efforts. Seven points were added to each of our scores. And so, for the first time, the very thing I had been aiming to avoid became inescapable: a crucial conundrum was staring me in the face! The fact that I had a slight advantage over Jack meant that he had to solve it to win. If the thirty seconds expired without either of us solving the conundrum I would scrape home.

Richard made sure that we were prepared for the challenge, with our fingers poised on our buzzers, before asking for the conundrum to be revealed.

'AMENUTREE' appeared on the monitor. It meant absolutely nothing to me! The absence of any sound from Jack's direction gave me some encouragement: this was a difficult one and he was struggling too. I realised that there were three 'e's: this meant it was a word I would have bypassed when selecting nines for inclusion on the practice 'squares' on the grounds that it was unlikely to feature in a letters game. I carried on speculating with parts of words which could be formed from the letters I was contemplating. The ending '-ate' stood out as a possibility. About halfway through the allotted time I noticed the eight-letter word 'numerate', and wondered how to incorporate the remaining 'e'. I saw the possibility of adding it on the front, but dismissed it! I was thinking of the opposite of 'numerate', which I was fairly sure was 'innumerate'. The time was running out now, and I was almost home and dry. But I wanted to finish the game on a positive note. Even as I was shaking my head in acknowledgement that the conundrum had left me flummoxed it dawned on me that I might as well find out whether the opposite of 'numerate' might actually be 'enumerate'. With only one second remaining, Jack was unlikely to be able to come up with an answer if it turned out that mine was indeed wrong. So just before the music came to an end, I pressed my buzzer.

Shocked, Richard asked me for my answer.

'I don't think it is,' I began. 'Enumerate.'

Richard looked agitated, as though uncertain as to what, if anything, I was actually declaring. 'You say you don't think it is,' he began, 'but you've given me a word . . . just give me the word.'

83

'Enumerate,' I repeated, a little more positively. I looked towards the board as the answer was revealed, and only then did I realise that what I had come up with was actually a verb - to enumerate!

I sat back, feeling very relieved as the audience applauded. Richard commiserated with Jack, who admitted that he was 'absolutely devastated', yet had the grace to say that I had played really well.

A place in the final beckoned. In the 'hot seat', my opponent to be, Paul Gallen looked confident. Prompted by Richard, Paul stated that he had spotted the conundrum. Not surprisingly, he affirmed that this occurred before my 29th-second intervention. Richard enquired further about the last numbers game. Paul hadn't seen a solution to this, but then as far as I can tell it was impossible to get closer than we did. I wasn't unduly troubled by the upbeat tone of Paul's responses. I was feeling too excited about surviving this close encounter with such a talented player as Jack!

Chapter 9: 'You couldn't write the script!'

One of my goals had now been achieved: by securing a maximum possible eleventh appearance in series 52, I had ensured the greatest number of opportunities to publicise my novel. That morning, in anticipation of my appearance in the quarter-final, I had asked Damian Eadie whether it would be possible to feature the book in the preliminaries to the show. He had said that advertising it in this way would be going beyond what he was permitted to do. However, at the start of the final, Richard - unprompted by me - held up his copy of the novel to the camera and recommended it to the audience.

I felt really proud, and satisfied that everything I had done had been well worthwhile, irrespective of the outcome of the final.

Immediately before going from the Green Room to the studio Sue had given me her final words of support: 'You can do this,' she said. 'I know,' I assured her. I didn't really have a strong feeling either way about whether I *would* actually win: the one thing I did feel confident about was that it would be close.

Richard began the preamble by describing how two thousand people had applied for the series. He added that around fifty of them had got through, and that now there were just two left. When he went on to say that we had both played ten times, and both won ten times, my heart swelled with pride. I felt so thrilled to be involved in the occasion, that when Richard called for the audience to welcome us I was beaming with delight! Richard described my semi-final game with Jack as 'one of the all time greats'.

Richard then introduced Paul, elaborating on his semi-final triumph, noting in particular the remarkable fifty-point lead which Paul had established early in the game.

Turning to Dictionary Corner, Richard made reference to a 'man at the height of his powers', before clarifying that this was the reason why Richard Digance and Susie Dent were lucky to be working with *him*!

Paul had won the toss and chosen the challenger's chair. It therefore fell to me to make the first choice of letters. I began by saying hello to Carol 'for the last time'. Carol returned the greeting in a way which suggested she was feeling a sense of anticipation about the occasion. The first set of letters developed well: 'entails' sprang to mind immediately, but as the seconds ticked by I was able to better this with 'salivate'. Paul had the same word and we were both off the mark with eight points.

In round two the rare instance of two 'f's in the same selection threw me. I found it difficult to get beyond the five-letter word 'faces', although late in the thirty seconds I managed to find a six in the form of 'caries'. I doubted whether it would be enough. I was right: Paul had seen the seven-letter word 'fiacres'.

Richard was quick to spot that it was a word that Paul knew as a result of its appearances on the programme, rather than one which formed part of his normal vocabulary.

'You don't know what they are, do you?' he jested.

Susie explained that 'fiacres' were horse-drawn carriages.

My next selection of letters presented me with a dilemma. I had seen the word 'aperient': however the remaining letter was a second 'p', which triggered in my mind the possibility that the correct spelling might be *'apperient'*. As I was unable to dispel my uncertainty I opted instead to stick with the safe seven-letter word 'painter'. Paul declared the same word, and the scores moved on to 22:15 in his favour. Susie confirmed that my initial inclination towards the spelling of 'aperient' had, in fact, been correct.

Would I have cause to regret that I had passed over an opportunity to take the lead? What happened in round four suggested I might. I spent much of the thirty seconds unable to get beyond the six-letter word 'bigots', but then saw the seven-letter word 'moisten' to give myself hope that I would at least share the points. But Paul had an 'eight' in the form of 'mitogens'. It was an excellent spot, and I congratulated him on it.

Now I had slipped 15 points behind. The next round entailed my numbers selection, and I knew I had to take the opportunity this presented to try to get back within striking distance. I asked for a favourite combination: three large and three small numbers. Carol picked out the numbers (25, 50, 75, 1, 3 and 4) - despite getting them tangled up with some feathers from the decorations surrounding the numbers board - and a challenging target of 804 came up. It was easy enough to get 800, but the question of how to home in on the extra 4 remained. Suddenly the realisation that 804 was a multiple of 4 put a different light on the equation, and I soon found the necessary 201 ($\{3 \times 50\} + \{75\text{-}25\} + 1$). I managed to finish writing down my calculations with a few seconds to spare. Paul declared 803, and returned the compliment I had paid him at the end of the previous round as I reduced his lead to five points. Richard Digance brought the first 'half' to a close with a poem of a festive nature.

The next letters selection brought the letter 'q' out. I saw 'equators' and was fairly confident that this was acceptable, but then spotted 'quaestor' - a Roman word for 'treasurer' which I had come across in the course of my preparation, and felt more certain that this would be allowed. When Paul declared 'equators' the legitimacy of the word was confirmed, and we both added eight points to our scores. Richard was full of admiration for the fact that we had produced two eight-letter words containing the letter 'q'.

After round seven it was Richard Digance who came out with a complimentary remark: when both Paul and I saw the word 'hounds' from an unpromising selection, he added that he 'couldn't do better than the two geniuses here'.

Round eight provided another tie, this time with the word 'limited'. I had toyed with the possibility of '*tidyline*': I think I must have been mixing up 'tideline' and 'bodyline'. Paul and I shared the points in round nine as well with 'roomed'. Again Dictionary Corner had nothing more to offer, prompting Richard Digance to offer an assurance that they were doing their best!

Paul then opted for one large and five small numbers, but the target of 475 wasn't easy to obtain. The presence of the 75 wasn't particularly helpful, as 475 is not a multiple of 75. Paul got round it by calculating 400 from the small numbers and adding the 75. My solution was to divide the 75 by 3 to make 25, and multiply this by 19 created from the remaining small numbers. Carol remarked that we had come up with two really strange ways of doing it!

At the second interval the scores stood at 67:62. Round eleven saw a sixth consecutive tie: Paul had 'uprated', while I produced 'pirated'.

Paul's final choice of letters followed. Early in the thirty seconds I spotted the prefix 'inter-'. The remaining four letters could be combined to add '-nets': this was a nine-letter word! The video of the game clearly shows me wrestling with a dilemma: I was in no doubt that '*internet*' was in the dictionary, but would it be acceptable to pluralise the word? Theoretically it would be possible to have more than one, but I remembered the entry in the book as being immediately followed by 'the *internet*' in brackets; this inclined me to think that the lexicographers were emphasising the fact that there was only one '*internet*'.

I couldn't make up my mind what to do! It was Paul who declared first - he said simply 'eight'. The implications of what I decided were clear: if I went for a nine and it was there, the resulting eighteen points would put me thirteen ahead with three rounds remaining. If, however, I declared 'internets' and it was disallowed, Paul's eight would take him thirteen points clear! If I stuck with my 'safe' eight, I presumed that the five-point gap would be sustained. One thing was certain: the outcome of the game might well hinge on my decision.

Richard asked for my declaration: it was time to stop wavering! I suddenly found the courage to go for it. Once more I decided that if I was going to go down, I was going to go down bravely! The audience gasped as I said that I would 'try a nine'. I looked towards Susie as I uttered the word *'internets'*, expecting her to check the definition and weigh up the arguments for and against the plural form. But no: Susie responded straight away!

'It's capitalised, Mark,' she said apologetically.

I paused for a moment as I took this in; then I smiled at Susie as I appreciated the irony. I had been in such a quandary over whether the plural was legitimate; it hadn't crossed my mind that the question was irrelevant because the word itself would be disallowed!

The audience responded sympathetically. Richard remarked that it all added to the drama. Paul's word, 'interest' was sufficient to extend his lead. Two more tied rounds would assure him of victory prior to the conundrum.

My last selection of letters proved an awkward lot. This was exactly what I was hoping for: a combination yielding one of the 'regular' nine-letter words which we would both have seen straight away would have denied me the chance to close the gap. I saw the six-letter word 'mikado' (a Japanese emperor) about halfway through the thirty seconds, and was satisfied there was nothing better. Paul followed my declaration by saying that he would have to go for a six too. As soon as he revealed that he was trying the word '*miriad*' (as an alternative to 'myriad') I knew I was back in the game. Paul still led, but now the gap was down to seven points.

For the last numbers game Paul again asked for 'one large number and five small ones'. The target of 645 looked sure to be achievable: I saw a way of making 644 and wrote it down, wasting valuable time in the process. I looked again for 645, but had to admit defeat. I held my breath as Richard asked for Paul's declaration: if he hit the target the game was over, and I felt sure he would do just that! But Paul had also got stuck on 644: it turned out that our calculations were identical. It was left to Carol to show us what we could have done.

The scores moved on to 89 points to 82 in Paul's favour. Richard captured the tension of the moment expertly. Addressing the viewers, he expressed his hope that nobody disturbed them by phoning them up in the next two minutes. He then paved the way for the conundrum, asking for the lights to be dimmed, and reminding everyone that whoever got it would be the winner.

The moment of truth had arrived.

'GREATDRIP' came into view. I stared at it for a moment, not having the slightest idea as to what it might be, until the sound of Paul's buzzer made me sit upright. I waited to hear the solution to the conundrum. I had already accepted defeat.

Richard was flustered: having correctly identified that it was Paul who had pressed his buzzer, he momentarily said that it was actually me, before realising he had got it right the first time!

'No, sorry,' said Paul. 'I thought it was . . . '

It hadn't crossed my mind that Paul would get the conundrum wrong, but he had obviously realised that it wasn't what he first thought.

Even as Richard was awarding the rest of the time to me, I resumed my contemplation of the conundrum. I looked at the composition of 'GREATDRIP', and felt certain that the solution would be a word that was familiar to me. The combination of letters was such that it would have been an obvious candidate for inclusion on one of the 'squares' I had used to help me spot nines. It would therefore be one that I had practised. I had been thrown a lifeline: I felt confident that I would be able to seize it.

After just a couple more seconds I remembered that I had decided what to do in this situation. Taking my finger off the buzzer, I grabbed my pen and began writing down the letters in the form of a grid, just as I had done whenever Sue had sent me a text with a conundrum I didn't immediately recognise.

By the time I had completed the grid I had used about ten of the thirty seconds. I looked at the array of letters I had created, but still nothing sprang to mind. I thought it was likely that the word would begin with 'p', but couldn't get any further than that. So I tried looking for words ending in

'-ate' or '-ated', but this yielded nothing. I knew that time had to be running out: this was brought home to me by the theme tune, which I was normally able to ignore in my effort to maintain concentration. On this occasion I noticed an ominous change in its tone which suggested that the music was coming to an end. I was still clueless. I remember thinking that I would give it one last look, and that I would try words beginning with 'p' again. It struck me that the presence of a second 'r' was what made this word so tricky to spot. And then it dawned on me that I had struggled once before with a word on one of my 'squares' which began with a 'p' and contained two 'r's, and that the word concerned was 'partridge'. At once I realised that the letters on the grid were those required for 'partridge'! Although time was almost up, I snatched a glance at the monitor to check that the letters there confirmed my impression. Now I knew that the word was indeed 'partridge'! In a flash I realised that I had taken my finger off the buzzer. It suddenly seemed a long way away, and I was presented with the extra challenge of reconnecting with it and depressing it before the clock stopped. Luckily my finger caught it straight away, and the noise of my buzzer rang out across the studio.

I'll never forget the sound which came from the direction of the audience - a huge, collective gasp filled the air, as people aspirated their astonishment.

Richard was clearly taken aback too.

'Oh!' he exclaimed. 'Twenty-seven seconds to say what?'

'Partridge,' I replied, with a note of pride in my voice.

'Partridge in a pear tree,' enthused Richard. 'It's not partridge in a pear tree: it's partridge on the board!' As he spoke he revealed the answer, and the audience began to clap and cheer.

Unbeknown to me, Sue had found it impossible to watch the conundrum, and had buried her head in her hands. She had looked up momentarily when Paul's buzzer sounded, but had hidden her face again when the clock restarted. She was under the impression that either of us could still answer, so that even after I had buzzed she still didn't know whom the audience was applauding. It was left to Lisa to put her out of her misery by informing her that it was over, and that I had won.

The period of time I spent working out the conundrum went by very quickly. I was too busy concentrating to feel tense: it was only the response of the audience to the sound of my buzzer that alerted me to the electricity in the atmosphere! The thirty seconds must have seemed like an eternity for Paul. As I waited for him to recover sufficiently for the customary handshake, I tried to come up with something consolatory to say to him. All I could think of was 'Hard luck, mate'. Later, when Paul had shaken off his initial despondency and came over to congratulate me, I managed to convey my sympathy more articulately. I particularly remember assuring him that he would 'go on to do great things'. I reminded him that there would be a 'Champion of Champions' series at some point. Paul's father, Phil Gallen, also came up to offer his congratulations, which meant a lot to me.

Richard handled the immediate aftermath of the final with sensitivity towards both contestants. He commiserated with Paul straight away, and shook his hand in a gesture of conciliation. In congratulating me on my victory, Richard inadvertently made the comment which later inspired me to turn my experiences on Countdown into the book you are now reading.

'You couldn't write the script!' he exclaimed, before confirming that the final score was 92 points to 89, and that I was the winner.

There followed a break in the recording, which in the televised programme was filled by the customary compilation of highlights of the winner's 'career'. This was compiled with great care and skill by the editors, and featured some of the nine-letter words I had spotted: 'printhead', 'loftiness' and 'veronicas', as well as the moment when Carol was impressed by my hitting the target of 927 in the game against John Crocker. Also included was the occasion when Richard had remarked that I was 'becoming a bit of a beast' during the game against Ronnie, as well as an excerpt in which Jeremy Beadle observed with great enthusiasm that I was 'so good', and my reaction to the revelation that I had recorded the (joint) second highest score of all time in the game with John Gray. The tribute concluded with another extract from the game with John Crocker - the moment when I spotted the conundrum 'brilliant'.

When filming resumed, we mingled on the stage for the presentation. A round of applause was called for. Unaware that this was intended to form a link between the tribute sequence and the conclusion to the programme, I joined in - effectively clapping myself - until Richard stopped me!

Although Susie and Richard Digance were present, what followed was largely an exchange of good-humoured remarks between Richard and Carol, mingled with some reflection on the final itself.

Having assured me that 'we all love you', Richard again commiserated with Paul, asking him what he had thought the conundrum was when he buzzed; 'departing' was the reply. Carol revealed that when she had seen me scribbling, she had thought at first that I was just checking my answer. I affirmed that I had no idea at that point. Richard then asked me what I planned to do with the set of dictionaries I had won. Not realising that these would be delivered at a later date, I replied that initially I would put them in the boot of the car. The inference that I was actually going to store them there caused some amusement among the presenters. Carol concluded that the series had not been 'A Nightmare in *Paradise*', and Richard wished me good luck with the book. There were seasonal good wishes and farewell waves, and then the theme tune played; and so the final curtain fell on series 52 of Countdown - the series of which I had become overall champion, *my* series.

The photographer then shot numerous stills of combinations of those who had been involved in the show: some included Susie and Richard Digance, others featured just Carol and Richard with the finalists. There were some with Carol and Richard standing either side of me, others with just Paul and me, and finally some of me, alone with my prize. I had to hold one of the twenty volumes in my hands for some of these photos. In the end it felt like a slab of concrete, and I was glad to put it down again!

Carol and Susie said goodbye while we were still in the studio, but the rest of the Countdown team and most of the contestants made their way to the bar area for a reception.

Damian mentioned that the standard of this series was such that a number of the top players would be invited to the next Champion of Champions series. As this occurred during a conversation with Jack and me, I took it that we would both be invited. It made me feel really pleased that Jack would be able to put aside the disappointment of his semi-final defeat at my hands and look forward to a possible rematch. We also spoke with Richard for the last time. He congratulated me again on winning the final, and wanted to know more about Sue's experience of being in the audience. He told her that they hadn't ever had a final quite like it! Richard's parting comment was that he would see us again for the Champion of Champions series.

Some of those who were staying in the hotel for the night decided to eat out together that evening. Steve Moir recommended the pool hall across the road from the hotel, which did indeed have a good selection of food. His sister and grandmother had come down from Scotland for the occasion, and Sue and I joined them, along with Paul and his father, and had a memorable last evening in Leeds. Steve, Paul and I played pool some of the time. I had two games with Paul: I won the first one as a result of Paul potting the black ball prematurely, but then he got his revenge in the second game.

Chapter 10: Life and death

The following day, Thursday 11th November, we said our farewells at breakfast time, and made our way home. I returned to work on the Friday, and was immediately faced with an enquiry regarding how I had got on in the quarter-finals. As with most workplaces, news travelled fast within the depot, and there seemed little point in trying to keep it quiet for the benefit of anyone who might have wanted to watch the climax to the series unfold as if 'live'. The first person to ask how I had got on was Ray, a fellow Branch Direct driver, whose mother was a regular Countdown viewer. After that I hardly told anyone myself. Most people heard it on the grapevine, and offered their congratulations when they saw me.

As for my friends outside of work, it was a lot easier to keep them in the dark, and I continued to encourage them to watch the shows in order to see how I fared. The excitement began just a few days later, with the screening of my début game against Margaret. In the days that followed, it became commonplace for my mobile to go berserk at around 4.15pm, as people sent texts or rang to say 'Well done!'

I had wondered how it would feel to watch myself on television. Might I be horrified at the way I looked or sounded, I wondered? In the event, I felt quite reassured when I saw the shows. I was satisfied that I looked presentable, and that the shirts we had chosen blended well with the set. What I said came across clearly, and when I wasn't deep in concentration I smiled a lot! People who saw me endorsed this impression. A friend from my novelists' group in Brighton left a message saying that he had never seen anyone looking so at home on the programme. Some friends of my parents even suggested I ought to work as a television presenter! It was all very heartening, if a little flattering.

As the run of eight games drew to a close, my expectations of the effect on sales of 'A Nightmare in Paradise' increased. As there were only around a dozen bookshops which actually had copies on shelf, I would have to rely on people who went in person to their local stores, and on those who accessed Amazon. I had no idea what to expect in the way of volume of sales. As a precaution, I had contacted the printers to ascertain how quickly they would be able to run off extra copies should the remaining stock prove insufficient. There was a steady trickle in the wake of my initial appearances, but this subsided before the quarter-finals were due to be screened. Overall, it was a disappointing response. I was left hoping for better things from the screening of the finals of the series.

One person who contacted me via Countdown, wanting to buy a copy was George Stanhope, who entered into correspondence with me, and as a result became a friend. I also heard from my old school association, with whom I had lost contact. One of the group's members had seen me on the show, and had tracked down my address. Months later I received a very welcome phone call from Roger Davies, a teacher who had taught me Latin, and who was one of those responsible for instilling in me a passion for language.

The most remarkable correspondence came from a relative I didn't even know I had! Some of my ancestors, who had come to this country from Russia, changed their surname to Turner. My grandfather's brother was among them. His son Dudley, who coincidentally had once been a contestant on the show himself, initiated correspondence, from which I learned about a wing of the family I would otherwise never have heard of.

The week during which the final was to be screened soon came around. On my birthday Sue and I watched the video of my quarter-final appearance. Needless to say this was an exciting way to celebrate! During the evening after the semi-final was shown, I was at my novelists' group's pre-Christmas drink. The other novelists had been following my progress from the start, and were getting together to watch the final the following afternoon. I made sure I didn't spoil the occasion, by giving nothing away about the outcome.

On the morning of the final my local paper, the *Argus*, contacted Countdown asking to be put in touch with me. Charlotte Hudson rang me to check that I had no objection, and shortly afterwards I received a call from one of their reporters. They wanted to know all about my experiences on Countdown, particularly with regard to the final, of which they wanted to know the outcome. The *Argus* also sent a photographer round to my flat to take numerous photos of me. I chose to wear the blue Countdown sweatshirt which had formed part of the goody-bag which all contestants receive. The reporter compiled a very well written article, which appeared prominently in an issue early the following week. The article made reference to my novelistic activities, as I had requested, thus providing further free publicity for 'A Nightmare in *Paradise*'. Similar coverage was later furnished by work-related publications. Prompted by my manager at Branch Direct, a reporter from the Royal Mail's monthly in-house magazine, *The Courier*, contacted me to obtain details for an article. He also arranged for a photographer to visit the depot: I spent the best part of an hour assuming various poses in a spare van! A similar article was produced for the Communication Workers' Union publication, *The Voice*.

The series 52 final was screened during the afternoon of Friday 17th December. I was at work that afternoon, but luckily one of the breaks in my routine occurred shortly after the programme ended, so I was able to deal with the flurry of excited texts and calls which followed the dénouement. As Sue and I were both busy that evening, we didn't get to see the show until the next day. My uncle John, who had seen the show when it was transmitted, had told me that even though he and my aunt Julia knew the result they were on the edge of their seats. Even I felt far tenser watching the show subsequently than I had at the time! My explanation is that it's easier to be actively involved in the situation than it is to be an onlooker. It gave me some insight into how Sue must have felt at the time the contest was reaching its climax.

As I watched the televised version of the final, what mainly preoccupied me was whether the moment when Richard had held up his copy of my novel would be left in. I felt it was unlikely, given what Damian had told me about the programme's policy concerning advertising. My doubts proved to be well founded. I understood why, of course, but it was very disappointing from a career point of view. Orders for 'A Nightmare in *Paradise*' continued to come in steadily for several months after the final, but I estimated that I sold only an extra 100 copies as a result of the programme. I had around 500 left in stock at the time. Some of the remainder are still waiting to find an owner, but I am confident they will all do so eventually.

There was a further development with respect to my writing career, which ultimately ended in disappointment. I had found my preliminary work for my appearances on Countdown stimulating to the point where I was led to enquire about work as a lexicographer. I was aware that this was a very specialised field, with an appropriately small number of people in it. Nevertheless, I decided to write speculative letters to publishers, explaining my background and asking to be considered for any work that they might deem suitable. One of the replies I received was from one of the major publishers of dictionaries, Chambers. They were unable to offer any lexicographical work, but were keen to hear of any ideas for language-based books I might have. In fact, a couple of ideas for books had come to mind during the course of my preparation for Countdown, so I wrote back giving a brief outline of them. Shortly afterwards I had a reply which indicated an interest in the idea I had come up with for a book describing the plethora of words from other languages which have found their way into the English dictionary. I was asked to send a book proposal with sample text and a marketing plan. I produced a passage giving details of some of the Australian words which have enriched the language available to the modern English-speaker - words such as 'stickybeak' (an inquisitive and prying person) and 'drongo' (a stupid or incompetent person). When I submitted my proposals I was very hopeful that a commission would result. However, when I received the publisher's reply, I learned that they had decided not to proceed with the project on the basis that it would be difficult to find a suitable structure for the book, and to sustain a lively, informative approach.

The loss of this opportunity was a huge blow to my morale. Since the series 52 final my spirits and my expectations had been high. I had really come to believe that my Countdown victory represented a turning point in my attempt to establish myself as a writer. The outcome of the correspondence with Chambers brought me down to earth with a bump! I put the idea for the language book aside for the time being, although

I intend to take another look at its viability at some point in the future.

Soon after the end of the series, Sue and I were invited to a celebration of my Countdown victory held by our Colombian friends, Carlos and Lucy, whose eleven-year-old daughter Jessica had followed my progress on Countdown with great enthusiasm, as had her friend Sara. It turned out to be a hilarious occasion, involving a highly entertaining re-enactment of the show. Carlos dressed in a tie and jacket worthy of Richard himself, while our friend Martha performed Carol's role, even managing to copy the way Carol sometimes throws her hair back over her shoulder. The remaining guests took it in turns to compete with me at a round of Countdown. Sue surprised herself by getting a numbers game spot on! Another Colombian friend, Alfonso, made a video of the occasion, and some time later Sue and I spent another highly amusing evening reliving the occasion.

Early in January 2005, I learned from George Stanhope that a Countdown tournament was to be held in Lincoln. The event was organised by Ben Wilson, overall champion of series 46. Through George, I was able to put my name on the list of competitors. Some of the other participants' names were very familiar to me: among them were previous series champions Stewart Holden, Tom Hargreaves, and Chris Wills. Another name on the list would become very familiar in Countdown circles: Conor Travers.

It was great to meet some of those whom I had watched and admired in recent years. COLIN, as Countdown in Lincoln became known, was also the first opportunity Sue and I had to meet our new friend George in person. Games were played over nine rounds, and I managed to win the first five, which meant that I was involved in what was effectively the final with Chris Wills, who was also unbeaten. Sue was helping Ben's mother, who was kindly organising the refreshments, when I told her that I was going to be involved in the deciding match. 'Does that seem familiar to you?' I asked her, grinning as I spoke.

Chris took an early lead, producing an eight-letter word ('irritant'), which I missed. He then went further ahead by beating me on a numbers game. I was unable to respond, with the result that Chris took an unassailable lead into the last round, which featured a conundrum ('dentition') which neither of us managed to solve. So my luck had finally run out. I was nevertheless delighted to finish second in such illustrious company.

Moreover, a new challenge lay ahead. Shortly before COLIN took place, I had a letter from Damian Eadie, inviting me to take part in the next Champion of Champions Series, and once again I was determined to go all out to win. Filming was scheduled for May - just a few months after the series 52 final. Soon afterwards, details of the line-up came through: I was to compete against Stuart Earl, who had been a quarter-finalist in series 50. In the event of victory, a rematch with Paul Gallen was a possibility, if he were successful against series 51champion Stewart Holden. In the other half of the draw were series 49 champion John Davies, young Scottish genius Sweyne Kirkness, series 50 winner Chris Cummins and my semi-final opponent Jack Welsby.

There were some formidable competitors in the line-up, and I immediately set about my preparation, even though it seemed as though I had hardly finished working towards series 52! Whilst the Champion of Champions series was my main focus at this time, I had also embarked upon another quest: that of appearing on Channel 5's lunchtime quiz show, Brainteaser, which unfortunately has now been taken off the air. The format of the show was different from that of Countdown. Two pairs of contestants competed in word games and answered general knowledge questions, and the two winners played similar games to decide who would be the day's champion. The winner then took on the 'pyramid'. This was a puzzle which involved starting with a three-letter word and rearranging its letters, together with others introduced one at a time on the lines below, to form longer words. At the bottom of the pyramid was an eight-letter word. If the day's champion reached this point they collected the maximum of £3,000, although they could - and usually did - 'stick' with smaller amounts rather than risk losing it all by running out of time. Unlike Countdown, an appearance on Brainteaser was a one-off – each day's edition featured fresh contestants.

I had been watching Brainteaser for some months in the run-up to my appearances on Countdown. I found the word games stimulating and enjoyable, as well as being good practice for the letters games. Encouraged by the discovery during the finals of series 52 that Steve Moir had won the maximum prize on Brainteaser, I sent in an application form early in 2005. I received a call from Helen at Brainteaser just as Sue and I were getting into her car, and took a phone audition for the programme while we were in a multi-storey car park in Kingston. The audition involved answering some mostly straightforward general knowledge questions. I was given the news that I had passed the audition straight away. As Brainteaser was filmed in Bristol, I arranged to take part in a show a couple of months later, on a day when Sue and I were travelling to Cornwall to spend the weekend with my parents and grandmother.

In the meantime, I carried on watching and playing along with the show in much the same way as I had done for Countdown. The faster pace of Brainteaser makes it difficult to keep an accurate score, but my overall impression was that most of the time I would have outscored the other contestants to become the day's champion, and that more often than not I would have gone on to reach the bottom of the pyramid.

On one occasion I switched on the video and got a surprise: Jack Welsby was among the day's contestants. I was really pleased when he went on to win the maximum prize. Jack's success also boosted my confidence with regard to Brainteaser. My main concern was the general knowledge element. A lot of the questions concerned soap operas, about which I knew nothing at all! Other subjects which came up regularly were films and famous people. I rarely go to the cinema, and have limited knowledge of celebrities. If the wrong questions came up, I would be forced to rely heavily on my skill at the word games.

We arrived at the studio on the morning of Friday 22nd April. We were shown to the Green Room, where we met the other contestants and their partners. Later Alex Lovell, Brainteaser's presenter, came in and chatted to us. She was very bubbly and friendly. We then went through to the recording studio for a rehearsal. The room was much smaller than that used for Countdown, and there was no studio audience. Even the contestants' partners had to remain in the Green Room.

The rehearsal involved running through our profiles, and having a try at each of the three games which the initial pairs were to play. Two of these were word games, and one was a test of general knowledge. The person I was paired with was Martin, a singer who also worked as an extra. Although I had the edge over him in the letters games, he was in the ascendancy in the general knowledge round. We were given five questions: Martin knew the answers to all of them, and I knew none!

We returned to the Green Room to await the start of the show. I didn't know at that point whether I would be competing against Martin or one of the other contestants, Ann and Louise. I actually hoped I would meet Martin in the first round. My reasoning was that the games the two winners went on to play involved a proportionately higher general knowledge element. If Martin and I were to meet at that point I might not only lose - I might be humiliated! Luckily I got my wish: I was drawn against Martin in the first pairing of the day.

The fact that Brainteaser was transmitted live meant that it was run to a tight schedule. At exactly 1pm we went live on air. Alex began by enquiring about my work as a novelist. In the rehearsal she had asked me what the title of the book was. I assumed she would do so again, but she didn't, and I wasn't sharp enough to ensure that it featured in our brief conversation. An opportunity was squandered, and consequently as far as I know I sold only one copy of 'A Nightmare in *Paradise*' in consequence of my appearance on Brainteaser.

The first game, entitled Scramble, involved rearranging words which had been chopped up and the resulting chunks placed in the wrong order. Unlike Countdown, the contestants stood and looked towards a monitor several yards away. I found this rather difficult; and, although I wasn't aware of it, I was clearly squinting in order to see the letters clearly. Nevertheless I managed to get most of the words right, and was leading by 50 points to 5 at the end of the round. Nevertheless, I was taking nothing for granted - despite Martin's comment that he would 'get his coat' at this point! The general knowledge round which followed was much more even, but I actually extended my lead to 110 points to 45. At this point Martin seemed to give up, and in the ensuing letters game (which involved coming up with words containing three particular letters in a given order) he appeared to let me get on with it. As a result I was able to amass a total of 180 points.

I took a back seat and watched the game between Ann and Louise, both of whom were lively characters. It was Ann's birthday, but Louise was the one to celebrate a comfortable victory, giving her the opportunity to play me to see who would take on the pyramid.

The first round was a general knowledge contest, which entailed being the first to guess a person, place or object, as up to four clues were gradually revealed. I was very pleased to get to the end of this round with the scores level, despite the presence of two questions about television serials, one of which I actually managed to answer, solely because Sue had happened to mention the programme concerned ('Supernanny') in a conversation we had had shortly beforehand on the subject of children's behaviour!

Another word game would decide the contest: this time the objective was to come up with a word of specified length, with the first and last letters given. Here I felt on more solid ground, and managed to open up a lead over Louise that enabled me to clinch victory by 80 points to 50.

I had become the day's champion, and was assured of at least £100. A short commercial break preceded my attempt to win considerably more. Alex reminded me that it was important when attempting to work through the pyramid to articulate your thoughts, so that her responses could be more helpful. Whereas when trying to solve a conundrum on Countdown, only one attempt is permitted, on Brainteaser any number of guesses would be allowed within the 45 seconds set aside for the challenge.

I composed myself and looked at the initial three-letter word: one. The clock began ticking, and an 'n' was added at the end of the row below. The only combination I could see was the word 'neon'. This was correct. I had used just one second and my winnings had increased to £200. From this point on, failure to spot the word on the line below mean that the sum would revert to £100. I had no intention of opting out. I was determined to get to the bottom of the pyramid!

Before the next letter was added, it occurred to me that the next word was likely to be 'tonne'. When a 't' appeared in the first space I was able to say this word without using up another second on the clock.

I guessed the next word might be 'bonnet'. When an 's' appeared in the first space, my reaction was to go instead for 'sonnet'. This proved to be correct too - and again I was quick enough not to have slipped below 44 seconds! My winnings stood at £750.

In the short time available to me before the letter on the line below was revealed, I could only see one word that contained all the letters in 'sonnet' and one other letter, and that was 'tension'. When an 'i' appeared in the middle of the line, I was again quick off the mark. Once more I was correct. Alex exclaimed: 'Just look at that clock, Mark!' Unbelievably, it was still showing that I had used just one second.

Alex asked me whether I could see a word that would fit on the bottom line. I replied that I could: I was considering the eight-letter word 'noisiest'. But even as I spoke I realised that this couldn't be right. There was only one 'n' in 'noisiest', whereas there were two in 'tension'. I had so far won £1,500. I had promised Sue that if I did really well I would pay for us to have a romantic holiday. I already had enough to achieve this. If I carried on to no avail it would all go out of the window! Nevertheless, with so much time in hand there was no way I was going to do anything other than play for the maximum prize!

'Are you this good at home?' Alex enquired. I was already focused on the monitor. I muttered something about possibly not being quite as good; Alex complimented me on my ability to work under pressure. The final letter appeared: it was an 'l' in the fourth of the eight positions. Nothing sprang to mind, so I began experimenting aloud with possible combinations of letters. What I came out with sounded like total gibberish! But I didn't care. It was the best way to pick up some clues as to whether I was getting close to unravelling the word.

For nearly thirty seconds I was getting nowhere. Suddenly I hit upon the idea that the word might start with 'in-'. I had noticed that when Alex was aware that contestants were barking up the wrong tree she made suggestions like: 'try something else'. She stayed quiet, which boosted my confidence that I was thinking along the right lines. With just fifteen seconds remaining, I hit upon a word, although it took a couple of attempts for me to pronounce it properly! 'Insolent' I declared.

'Yes!' cried Alex. I rolled my eyes and smiled with relief. I had won £3,000! Moments later the show was over. Alex came over and gave me a congratulatory hug. The photographer was brought in to capture the moment, in case of media interest (I don't know whether any actually resulted). I returned to the Green Room, where Sue was beaming. She had been watching the finale with Louise's husband, John. He had put aside his disappointment about the outcome of my game with Louise, and was sportingly cheering me on.

Soon we were bound for Cornwall. We decided to take the scenic route, partly because we wanted to avoid the Friday afternoon rush hour traffic, but also out of curiosity, as neither of us was familiar with the coastal route. It turned out to be a long journey along undulating roads. But we didn't mind; we were too delighted about my win to grumble. A cheque came through my letterbox a few days later, and we later had a wonderful week in the Sardinian resort of Villasimius.

It seemed that there was no looking back: the next stop was our return visit to Leeds. During the couple of weeks remaining before the Champion of Champions series, I concentrated on my preparations. On the morning of Friday 6th May I packed my case in readiness for the journey, which we were going to make over the weekend, as filming was due to begin on the Monday lunchtime. While I was at work that day, I picked up a message which Charlotte Hudson had left on my landline: Richard Whiteley had been taken ill, and would be unable to work next week. The series would be rearranged for a date later in the year. The postponement of the series at short notice was hugely disappointing – however, I immediately resolved to use the extra time to increase my chances of success.

When I rang back to acknowledge that I had received the message, I expressed my hope that Richard wasn't too poorly. At that stage it was believed that he had come down with 'flu. It turned out that he had in fact contracted pneumonia. Still, all the news I heard suggested that he would recover. It seemed that there would be a need for a 'stand-in' presenter. A few weeks later Sue and I went to see Richard Digance, who was performing his musical comedy routine in the Dorking Halls. During the show Richard announced that he had been asked to act as host of Countdown, and that he would be going to Leeds to film the first shows of the new series at the beginning of July. Even then we had no inkling that Richard Whiteley was so close to death. On the evening of Sunday 26th June my mother sent me an article she had seen in her newspaper, which said that Richard was recovering, following heart surgery. Minutes later I happened to switch to the Teletext when a headline appeared: Richard Whiteley was dead. Complications resulting from pneumonia had taken too great a toll on his heart.

I felt shocked to receive this news, so soon after hearing the encouraging report from my mother, and saddened that someone who had been part of my life for so long, and who had presided over one of my happiest moments, was no longer there. I really felt that I had lost a friend. Later that evening I broke the news to Sue, who also felt a sense of loss.

Richard's death coincided with the last few programmes of series 53. The first transmission was postponed, but by the Friday of the following week the remaining shows, which had been recorded just before Richard was taken ill, had all been broadcast. The final was preceded by a programme in which Carol and Susie, along with celebrities who had featured in Dictionary Corner, paid tribute to Richard. I'll always remember Carol's parting comment: 'The clock stopped too soon'.

It was fitting that the series 53 final, between John Mayhew and John Brackstone, should be a classic encounter. After the lead had changed hands more than once, the scores were level with just the conundrum remaining. When neither contestant was able to convert ARTGENIUS into 'signature', a second conundrum was produced, and this time John Mayhew spotted 'falsified' straight away, to become not only series champion but the winner of the last show ever presented by Richard Whiteley.

Chapter 11: Countdown's future is secured

The question as to whether it would be the end of the programme remained. People frequently asked *me* what was going to happen! I hadn't heard anything through the media, so I logged on to Channel 4's Countdown website. Here I found reference to an official statement, which turned out to be an accurate account of what eventually happened. The programme would be taken off the air for the rest of the summer, but would return in the autumn once a new presenter had been appointed. In the meantime, I heard various rumours: Carol was going to leave, Noel Edmonds had been approached, and the one that proved well founded - Des Lynam was going to be the new presenter. As news of Des's appointment became more widespread, I called the Countdown team to ask about future plans for the show. They confirmed that the return of the show was imminent, but there were no plans for a Champion of Champions series at present. Moreover, in view of the fact that the contestants would be from the era prior to Richard's death, there was a chance that it might be deemed inappropriate for it to happen at all.

It was disheartening news. I had continued practising, even while the programme was off the air, on the basis that I was likely to be called back at some point. Now I was unsure whether there would be any point in carrying on. Nevertheless, I was determined to keep going until there was definitive news.

When the new series got under way I was surprised by the buoyancy of the mood on the set. When I reflected on it, I realised that it was just how Richard would have wanted it. I knew that it must have been really difficult, especially for Carol and Susie, to be upbeat at this time, but they achieved it with characteristic professionalism. Although Des had a hard act to follow, and was clearly very nervous initially, he soon settled in, and added his own brand of humour to the show. Series 54 turned out to be a great success, not least because it saw the emergence of a true star, in the form of the youngest ever series champion, Conor Travers. When first introducing him, Des said he had been told that Conor was very good at the game. Even those of us who had taken part in the Lincoln tournament earlier in the year, in which Conor came 17th, had little idea how adept he had become in the meantime. Conor coasted through eight games and amassed 890 points, in the process of becoming number one seed.

I decided to call the Countdown team again for an update about the likelihood of a Champion of Champions series. I held my breath while Marie conferred with Damian. When the reply came it was good news: there was definitely going to be a Champion of Champions series, although no decision had been taken as to when it would be.

Around this time I managed to improve on my best ever score while playing along to a game at home. It happened during a remarkable show which featured five nine-letter words: 'transomed', 'policeman', 'triangles' (or 'integrals'/'gnarliest'), 'motorises', and 'gesneriad'. I spotted all five, but I failed to score in four of the other ten rounds! I had reached 141 after the last letters game, surpassing my previous best by 3 points. A tricky numbers game, and then an unusually hard conundrum ('reticence') dashed my hopes of adding to my tally. Still, I was encouraged by my performances at home during series 54. Things would have been very close if I had been involved in any of Conor's games: I would have won four out of eight, including a couple of games where I had to be lightning-quick with the conundrums.

Early in January 2006, I learned that Ben Wilson was organising another Countdown event in Lincoln. By coincidence, I was intending to visit George in Boston at the time, so we agreed to take part again. As in the previous year, there was some tough opposition: Chris Wills, Stewart Holden, Kirk Bevins and Conor Travers were among the contenders.

After winning four hard-fought games, including one - against Jerry Humphreys - which went to a crucial conundrum, I found myself grouped with the other two unbeaten players, Kirk and Conor. The format of COLIN is that each of the three players takes a turn at 'being Carol' while the other two compete. Conor and I played first. The young genius had already taken one notable scalp, that of Chris Wills, who commented: 'I lost to Conor - but then, who doesn't?' I had also witnessed Conor notice a nine-letter word, 'impulsion', from a set of letters which were on a table nearby: what made this more impressive was that from where he was standing, the letters were upside-down!

It came as no surprise when I struggled against the youngster. A couple of obscure words ('lariat' and 'hyalite') were sufficient to end my winning streak, although I was able to make the scores close by unravelling the conundrum, 'vestibule'.

My game with Kirk followed, and was a really close contest. I held a slender lead until I missed a fairly easy solution to a numbers game, so handing Kirk the advantage with just the conundrum remaining. What followed brought back memories of my series 52 final. Some of the conundrums Ben had provided contained the letters in the name of the tournament. One of these was 'COLINDART'. It meant nothing to me. After about ten seconds I scribbled down the letters; I could hear Kirk doing likewise. In the nick of time the word 'doctrinal' sprang to mind, enabling me to snatch an unlikely victory.

It looked as though Conor was going to coast to a sixth victory when he opened up a healthy lead over Kirk. But a great comeback ensued, and this time it fell to Kirk to see the crucial conundrum ('gradation') with only seconds to spare. All three of us had ended up on five wins. I had the highest points total, but Chris Wills and Stewart Holden had also gone on to notch up five successes, and in so doing had accumulated more points than me. Chris deservedly claimed victory at COLIN for the second year in succession.

An amusing moment occurred during the presentations which followed. Damian Eadie had kindly provided a prestigious Countdown teapot, to be awarded to the highest placed contestant who wasn't already in possession of one from their exploits on the programme. This honour fell to Kirk, who had finished fifth, just behind Conor on points. It had been Kirk's misfortune to take on series 51 octavian Richard Pay at a time when the latter was in full flow, and to have left the studio without a victory to his name. As Kirk proudly collected his teapot, I noticed that it looked a bit wobbly.

'Don't drop it!' I called to him: but I had hardly finished speaking when there was a crash. The lid had come off and fallen to the floor! Kirk examined his prize anxiously. Luckily it was undamaged. It would have been a great shame if a moment he had waited so long for had ended in calamity!

Afterwards I reflected on the day's games: for the most part I was satisfied with the way I had played. I still needed to improve my knowledge of obscure words, but I had come up with some well thought-out solutions in numbers games, and solved all six conundrums. Had I not been challenged during the game against Jerry and so discovered – to my amazement -that '*unraced*' was not permissible I would have been level on points with Chris. The fact that it was all so very close gave me grounds for optimism with regard to the Champion of Champions series, whenever it might occur. I felt sure I had reached a higher standard than when I won series 52; and I was certain I was capable of further improvement!

Chapter 12: 'It's like the good old days again!'

I often miss calls on my mobile, as I spend much of my time on the road. This happened one morning late in February 2006. When the call record showed 'number withheld' I assumed that the voicemail message that was left would be of an official nature. I certainly didn't expect that it would bring news I had been longing to hear for months. How wrong I was! As soon as I heard Damian Eadie's voice I guessed why he was ringing me. It transpired that the long-awaited Champion of Champions series was to be filmed in late April. I had two months in which to prepare! I rang Damian straight away and confirmed my availability.

For some weeks there was considerable doubt as to whether Sue would be able to come with me at all. Her younger son had broken his ankle go-karting just after Christmas. Following several setbacks during the recovery period, and the worry that went with them, Sue felt that he might still need her close at hand when the Champion of Champions series was due to take place.

Shortly after the call from Damian, the recording dates were confirmed, and soon afterwards the details of the draw came through. I discovered that I was in the first game, and so knew that defeat would mean I would be the first person to be eliminated from the competition. I saw that I had been paired with Steve Graston, whom I knew had given Stewart Holden a close game in the final of Series 51. Some stiff competition awaited the winner: Matt Shore, who had been impressive in the preliminary rounds of series 54 (still in progress at the time), or Chris Cummins, unbeaten winner of series 50.

Whoever emerged victorious from that group would face one of a fearsome foursome: John O'Neil (whom I will refer to as Jono hereafter), Jack Welsby, John Mayhew, and Paul Howe. Jono, whose prowess at the numbers games is quite legendary in Countdown circles, had the misfortune to lose his series 53 semi-final against eventual champion John Mayhew by a single point. It looked likely to be a close call as to who would triumph between him and Jack. Paul Howe had shown more than enough ability in series 54 to suggest that he would be a match for John Mayhew. If I got through my first two rounds, there would be a tough task ahead of me in the semi-final. The one consolation was that Conor was in the other half of the draw, meaning that I would face him only if we had both done well enough to make it to the final.

Conor's first round opponent was to be John Hunt - fourth seed in my series and renowned for his wizardry with six small numbers. The winner would face either John Brackstone, runner-up in series 53, or David Wilson, runner-up in series 49. In the remaining quarter of the draw, series 49 champion John Davis was to play Gary Male, semifinalist in series 51. The winner of that match would face either Paul Gallen or Eammon Timmins, who reached the final of series 50.

There would be at least four competitors with unbeaten records: John Davis, John Mayhew, Chris Cummins and myself. Assuming the series 54 winner came from among the trio of Conor, Matt and Paul Howe, then there would be five of us with eleven wins from eleven games. At least four of us were sure to taste defeat for the first time.

One notable absentee was Stewart Holden, who would have been a serious contender. Unfortunately for him, he was unavailable at the time of recording.

The Champion of Champions Series would see the introduction of a new edition of the *Oxford Dictionary of English* (*ODE*). Damian emailed all the contestants with a list of the changes. There were several hundred new words, and just a handful of deletions. By now my much used and widely travelled *ODE* was literally falling apart. The cover had come off and the pages at either end (containing the introductory notes and the appendices) were gradually liberating themselves from the main body of the text! When I discovered that the page listing chemical elements was about to detach itself, I salvaged it and put it on the kitchen worktop next to the kettle, allowing me to glance at it whenever I made myself a coffee. It worked: when 'astatine' (number 85) came up in an early game, I spotted it straight away!

When I saw that Damian's list of changes was substantial it was clear that it was time to get hold of the new edition, so I went into Brighton, and picked up a copy. I began to go through it, in conjunction with a copy of the update. This was useful, because in Damian's email the newly included words were simply listed alphabetically, without any explanation or indication as to whether they were nouns, verbs or adjectives. Ironically, as far as I'm aware only one of these words ('euroland') actually came up during the Champion of Champions series, but there were many that could easily have appeared, and which will no doubt get their turn on the show at some point. Anyway, it was important for my self-assurance for me to take the update on board.

As I went through the revised dictionary I fulfilled other objectives I had set myself. To this end I used different coloured highlighters to mark (among other things) words with a high vowel content, rarely used verbs, and words ending '-ee'. The further I got through the dictionary, the more it became apparent that there was still a large number of words which looked totally unfamiliar, even though I must have seen them several times before. As the Champion of Champions series approached, I decided I would have to go right through the whole dictionary one more time.

The recordings were to take place between Tuesday 25th and Thursday 27th April. Sue and I had kept the weekend immediately beforehand mostly free, to allow time for final preparations, and I managed to add the Friday before the weekend to my time off work. In the four days immediately prior to the Champion of Champions series I compiled a list of around 1,500 unknown words, recorded them on my dictaphone, and managed to play it through three or four times. The last occasion was on the final morning before filming. It took about half an hour to hear the whole recording from start to finish, and I was running out of time. So I put the dictaphone in the breast pocket of my shirt and carried on listening whilst I moved around the hotel room getting ready!

Of all the words on this list, I used just one (duchies), although several others came up in other shows. Nevertheless, from the point of view of focusing on the task in hand, it was a really worthwhile exercise. I remember showing the list to John Mayhew in the bar just after the conclusion of the Champion of Champions series. He seemed quite astonished that I had done so much preparation. I didn't think to mention that what he had seen was just the tip of the iceberg!

Happily, Sue's son had recovered sufficiently for her to travel, but her commitments were such that she was unable to accompany me to Leeds on the Monday. She would have to miss the whole of Tuesday's filming, and join me at lunchtime on Wednesday. This meant that she wouldn't be there for my game with Steve Graston. We knew that if I lost she wouldn't see me in action at all, and we would have to get over our disappointment separately until the following day. However, if I won, she would be able to make it to the studio in time for the quarter-final on the Wednesday. We agreed on a coded text with which I would let her know the result of Tuesday's game: XX if I lost, XXX if I won. Because of the situation, I was conscious of a degree of pressure before the opening game, which I had not felt before on the show. Perhaps it showed: afterwards Damian said to me that I seemed tenser than I had during series 52. However, I don't think that my performance was affected adversely by nerves. In fact it made me wonder whether I might actually have been too relaxed previously!

I drove to Leeds during the daytime of Monday 24th. The forthcoming challenge was clearly on my mind on the journey north: on the M1 I remember noticing a van marked 'DOGWARDEN', and it occurred to me that this was a potential conundrum for 'downgrade'! I arrived in time to catch most of the day's episode of Countdown: I was in good form, missing just one maximum score. For the rest of the day I stayed in the hotel, looking through the new dictionary, and listening to my dictaphone recordings. The only person I saw was Jono, with whom I had a brief chat as I came out of a lift. I was content to spend the time quietly, and leave the socialising for the next day when the contestants would converge on the Television Centre.

On the Tuesday morning I walked into Leeds and picked up some provisions. Finding the way into the city centre and back to the hotel proved something of a challenge, as it was necessary to thread my way through a network of main roads, flyovers, and large buildings. I took Sue's advice and refrained from doing any last-minute preparation, in order to keep my mind fresh for the afternoon's endeavours.

I strolled down to the studio in good time for 12.30pm, arriving at the same time as Conor and his father, with whom I exchanged greetings. Those already seated in reception included Eamonn Timmins and David Wilson, both of whom I remembered from their time on the show, but had never met in person before. I also met my opponent, Steve Graston, and his wife Michelle, for the first time, and took an instant liking to them both. It made me feel better, because if I was going to lose I wanted it to be to someone with whom I felt real affinity. I learned that our show was going to be transmitted on Steve's birthday. I felt a little bit uncomfortable, knowing that I might be about to spoil the occasion for him. I prefer achieving things which *don't* involve beating other people, such as setting a new personal best on a golf course. However, the nature of Countdown is such that someone will always end up disappointed. In reality, I think that most people who volunteer to appear on Countdown accept that the result may not go their way, and handle it well when it doesn't.

Gradually other competitors filtered in, and we were shown through to the Green Room. As the number of contestants was larger than usual, there were two dressing rooms in operation. There was no great urgency, as our recording wasn't scheduled to take place until 1.30pm, so there was time for us to catch up with people we already knew, and get acquainted with those we hadn't met before. I particularly remember series 49 champion John Davies bowling in. His unique - and rather amusing - way of breaking the ice was to go round the room identifying everyone by name, and reminding us of a good word we had come up with in the course of our appearances on Countdown: in my case it was 'loftiness' that he recalled.

I knew I could count on a warm reception from the Countdown staff. In particular, I'll always remember Lisa's greeting. 'It's Mark Tournoff!' she proclaimed. Lisa gave me a hug and told me she had loved reading my novel. I later learned that since series 52 Lisa had been promoted to floor manager. With her energy, organisational flare and communication skills, she had taken to the role like a duck to water.

It soon became apparent that there was going to be a delay, as an accident on the M6 had prevented some of the camera crew from reaching the studio on time. I didn't let this get to me at all, and I don't think it affected Steve either. It was around 2pm that we made our way to the studios. We were introduced to Des, and to Ron Atkinson, who was in Dictionary Corner for the day. Des immediately picked up on the fact that I lived in Hove, and told me he was going to point out that I was from 'Hove actually' - a phrase used in jest locally to allege a superior status to the residents of Brighton. He also wanted to know more about my writing activities. When filming began, I was introduced first, and was given the opportunity to mention 'A Nightmare in *Paradise*' again, and to say that 'Sharp Right to Oblivion' would be published later in the year. Steve was introduced as a commercial analyst for a shipping company from Liverpool. Carol then turned to Ron Atkinson, and teased him about the fact that he has his own football vocabulary, known as 'Ronglish'. Finally, Susie talked about the new edition of the *ODE*, mentioning some of the newly incorporated words; among them were 'bloviator', 'shroomer', 'retime' and 'retile'. And so the series got under way with my choice of letters.

I began by saying 'Hello again' to Carol, who replied, 'It's like the good old days again'. The first selection was an unpromising one, with a 'q' but no 'u'. I could manage no more than a six-letter word, 'mopers', which Steve matched with 'morose'. I later learned from 'The Countdown Corral' (an excellent website) that we could have had 'prosoma'. The next round produced seven-letter words: mine was 'unearth', while Steve spotted 'centaur'. Ron was impressed with the latter, which he and Susie hadn't seen. My selection followed: we both identified 'delists' and our scores moved on to 20 apiece. In the next round it was clear at once that the letters were very 'friendly', and the nine-letter word 'coastline' fell into place in my mind. I felt sure that Steve would see it too: but unfortunately for him he had only got as far as the eight-letter word 'toenails'. Ron provided the alternative nine, 'sectional'. I had opened up an eighteen-point lead, but it was not enough to defend at that stage, so I asked for 'three large numbers, and three small ones'. Carol remarked that she was in for a difficult three weeks! The target of 271 turned out to be relatively easy to reach, and our scores moved on to 48:30.

Ron then took the opportunity to tease Des by reminding him about a couple of occasions when his comments had backfired spectacularly. The first concerned the footballer Yakubu, whom Des had written off just before he scored a couple of spectacular goals. The other concerned Des's dismissal of Amberleigh House as too old and slow, shortly before the horse's Grand National victory. Carol observed that she would refer to any faux pas Des made in future as a 'Yakubu moment'.

The game resumed with Steve's selection of letters, from which we both saw 'jumper'. Dictionary Corner offered nothing better. However we learned later, from the competitors assembled in the Green Room, that everyone had overlooked the seven-letter 'gourmet' - a word which has appeared consistently on the show over the years.

Round seven provided another promising selection, from which I identified 'exordial', for eight points. It was the third time I had seen a derivative of exordium on the show! It was no wonder that, when Des asked me to define the word, I was able to give an explanation which Susie described as being 'by the book'. Ron revealed that there was another eight-letter word in 'darioles' (pots). My eight was enough to win the round, as Steve had declared a seven-letter word, 'derails'. In the following letters game, some giggling from the audience put me on the trail of 'randiest'. The presence of the 'z' suggested there was nothing better. Steve equalled my tally with 'strained'. The score was 70:46.

In round nine Steve matched my seven ('beneath') with 'methane'. He then asked for 'one large number and five small ones'. Carol's face lit up. 'I love you, Steve!' she declared. The target of 230 was indeed an easy one, so much so that Steve, Carol and I all found different ways of reaching it. At the interval I had reached 87 points and was 26 ahead. It was a decent lead, but one which could be overturned, particularly if Steve were to spot a nine-letter word, and I were to miss it. I set about defending my advantage with a five-vowel letters selection, thereby reducing the likelihood that it would yield a nine. We both spotted the seven-letter word, 'soapier', while Susie came up with 'aporias' (logical contradictions in an argument).

Steve's last choice of letters yielded some eight-letter words. I saw 'steading', while Steve had an anagram of this in 'sedating'. Ron added 'tangiest'. With three rounds left I was almost home and dry. I plumped for another five-vowel selection. The presence of a 'k' among the four consonants made it hard to find any decent words. I saw 'okapi', and thought that this might be the longest word available. But with a few seconds to go I noticed a very obscure word: 'ipomoea'. I wrote it down, but still couldn't really believe my eyes, so that when the time came to declare it I almost rejected it in favour of 'okapi'. Steve had declared a five, which meant that I couldn't be caught, even if I lost the round, and it was this realisation that gave me the confidence to go ahead with my declaration. To my surprise, even Susie looked bewildered! Des asked me to spell it, and Susie began to look it up. Des took the opportunity to ask me what the word meant. I remembered that it was a plant, although I couldn't have given details. Susie seemed quite overwhelmed that 'ipomoea' was indeed there. She explained that it was another name for a morning glory. I felt amazed that I had managed to find a word that Susie didn't know! It took my score on to 109.

Ron then made an observation, which unfortunately was edited out of the programme because of time constraints. Noticing my resemblance to the Chelsea manager (at that time) Jose Mourinho he commented: 'I've just realised something. He must win! He's the "Special One"!' I told him that people often remarked that I looked like Mourinho and recalled the occasion when Richard Whiteley had made this point, adding that Richard had - rather typically - got the manager's name wrong!

At this juncture I was under the impression that I had a chance of going through the whole fifteen rounds without missing anything (being unaware that I had earlier missed 'prosoma' and 'gourmet'). This possibility was in the forefront of my mind as Steve again asked for 'one large number and five small ones'. The target of 663, from a set of numbers including a 50, suggested that a solution might be produced by multiplying 13 by 51. Frustratingly, I couldn't find a way of achieving this (although I subsequently realised that it was in fact possible) and I resorted to other methods. The closest I could get was 659. Steve was closer with 662, and the seven points he gained took his score up to 83.

The conundrum remained. Although I knew that my passage to the quarter-final was secure, I was keen to extend my record of never having been beaten on the buzzer. When 'ELCRANIUM' was revealed, it didn't immediately fall into place. I saw that it was a combination of five different consonants and four different vowels, and therefore knew that it was a word I would have practised and should be able to discover. After ten seconds it came to me in a flash: it was 'numerical', and I pressed the buzzer almost without thinking!

My score moved on ten points to 119. The winning margin of 36 was more comfortable than I had expected, and didn't really reflect how close the game had been. Later Steve told me that he had run a sweepstake at work with respect to the number of points he would score against me, modestly dismissing the possibility that he might have beaten me! His score of 83 was towards the higher end of the scale, and he was pleased with his performance. Carol and Des were very complimentary about Steve's contribution, and a show which had been good-humoured and sporting came to a conclusion.

When we returned to the Green Room, we were greeted by a round of applause from the other contestants. Conor expressed his admiration for the fact that I had seen 'ipomoea', saying that he had never heard of it. I told him jokingly that I was counting on him to know it. Later Jack was equally fulsome in his praise, describing it as the 'spot of the century'.

Chapter 13: Keeping an eye on the talent!

As soon as I had the chance, I went outside and sent Sue the XXX message to signify that I had won. After that I settled down in the Green Room to watch the rest of the shows to be recorded that day. Before each show began, we received a visit from Sharon, who had stepped into the role vacated by Lisa's promotion, to ask who wanted to go into the studio and join the audience. I already knew my preference was to remain where I was. A number of the other contestants regularly stayed in the Green Room too: Matt, Conor, Paul Howe, Jono and Gary were among them. John Brackstone and his wife Cath were regulars as well. John Mayhew had suffered the misfortune of leaving his clothes on the train, and spent much of the first day in Leeds on an unscheduled shopping trip, but once he had returned he joined the group in the Green Room. Some of the other contestants alternated between the studio and the Green Room, while others, among them John Davies and Eamonn Timmins, preferred to ensconce themselves in the studio.

Those who spent most of their time in the Green Room got to know each other well, and a great sense of camaraderie developed among us. Matt, who has a lively sense of humour, contributed a lot towards the jovial atmosphere. While we were watching the games on the monitor, groupthink took over, and we all chipped in with words we had spotted, as well as any witty observations which sprang to mind. As the conundrums came up, whoever spotted the answer first called it out, often at the same time as the contestant on the show. Socially, it was a memorable few days, and I missed the other contestants' company when it was all over.

The second game involved John Davies and Gary Male. Early on, John established a healthy lead by spotting a nine-letter word, 'sealpoint'. He built on it by winning several more rounds. Towards the end of the game Gary tried a nine, '*greenouts*', which he clearly knew was a long shot. It was a valiant, but futile, attempt to close the gap. The final score was 106:73. Des commented that Gary was up against a good competitor; Gary concurred, and added that John was 'the best'. I had already concluded that John was a possible overall winner of the Champion of Champions series, but for me the person everyone had to beat was Conor. I had learned that Conor had, as expected, triumphed in the series 54 final. The next game would provide an indication of his form.

The teenager's opponent was to be John Hunt, whom I had seen briefly earlier in the day, and who had joked that he was looking for a swap so that he wouldn't have to play Conor. The apprehension wasn't entirely one-sided, however. Just before they went into the studio Conor asked John what it was worth not to choose six small numbers!

Conor went straight into the lead in their contest with 'emigrate', to John's 'frigate'. In round four, one of the only two combinations of letters which yield four nines ('creations', 'reactions', 'narcotise', and 'actioners') emerged. In the Green Room nobody doubted that both contestants would get nines. We speculated instead about which of the four choices they would go for: John had 'creations', whereas Conor opted for the less commonplace 'narcotise'. Only in round seven did Conor manage to extend his advantage, beating John's 'planter' with 'antelope'.

The second numbers game demonstrated that Conor's concern about John's propensity to select 'six little ones' was misguided. A target of 919 never looked achievable, but Conor was able to get closer with 918, to extend his advantage to 23 points. Four tied rounds at the start of the third part of the programme ensured victory for Conor. The youngster then rounded off an impressive performance by solving the conundrum at once ('toothless'), making the final score 124:91.

So far in the Champion of Champions series, three of us who had been overall series winners had booked our places in the quarter-finals, thus preserving our unbeaten records. The next game was between two players who had previously tasted defeat - albeit very narrowly - on the programme. Jack Welsby against Jono looked certain to be a game to savour. I was particularly looking forward to seeing them demonstrate their agility at the numbers games.

It was Jack who took an early lead by cleverly spotting 'amoebas' from a tricky selection of letters. In round three Jono had the distinction of being the first person to offer one of the words that had recently been included in the new dictionary: 'euroland', which coincidentally had been mentioned in a discussion in the Green Room earlier in the day. It was only enough to tie the round, as Jack had seen 'cauldron'. In the first numbers game Jono showed that he was as effective with selections of 'six small numbers' as he was with 'four from the top' by employing a cunning method of hitting the target of 718, involving creating 359 and multiplying it by 2. However, Jack was equally shrewd, and maintained a seven-point lead at the first interval.

Three tied letters games followed, before Jack increased his advantage with the obscure 'senarii' (the plural of 'senarius', a verse of six feet). Jono struck back when his first choice of numbers provided a difficult target of 818. Only Carol was able to find the exact figure, prompting Jono to observe that it was the first time she had beaten him when he had asked for 'four from the top'.

The match hung in the balance with five rounds remaining. Jack then extended his advantage to fifteen points with another excellent word ('tautened') in round eleven. When the next selection emerged a nine-letter word was on offer: 'prospered' seemed to shine out. In the Green Room John Brackstone saw it almost immediately. When Des asked for their declarations, I expected that at least one competitor would say 'Nine'. But I was wrong: 'reposed' was the best that either could produce.

Both contestants had squandered a great opportunity to change the complexion of the match: Jack could have secured victory in the game, while Jono could have come from behind to take a narrow lead.

The outcome of the game was still uncertain when Jono asked for his customary numbers selection in the penultimate game. 801 was another very tricky target. 800 was easy, but how could you get the extra one? We were enthralled to see whether either could manage to do it. When neither could, victory was assured for Jack. Carol again showed how it could be done. It fell to Jono to take some consolation by spotting the conundrum ('profanity') straight away, taking his final total to 94, leaving Jack on 99.

We had witnessed the first really close contest. It seemed certain that more would follow. In this respect, the last game of the day seemed a likely candidate. It started off that way. Paul Howe and John Mayhew had 37 points apiece at the first interval. What happened in the middle part of the show was remarkable: Paul took an eight-point lead in round six with 'samplers', to John's 'armless'. Round seven produced a tie: however, in the next letters game a nine came up. As with the previous show, it was spotted immediately backstage - this time by Conor, who added unhesitatingly that Paul would get it! I remember thinking how incredible it was that, as well as having an extraordinary vocabulary himself, Conor was so aware of his fellow competitors' strengths that he could confidently predict what they were likely to see! I was pleased that I saw 'geomatics' before anyone had revealed what the nine in question was. Conor was right: Paul had spotted it too. However, John was stuck on a seven with 'egotism'. As Susie read out the definition of 'geomatics' (the application of computerisation to geography), she admitted she had never heard of it.

Paul was suddenly 26 points ahead. As if to rub it in, he proceeded to win the next round with 'mordant', as well as the second numbers game, in which he was one closer to the target than John. I have rarely seen a game of Countdown transformed so completely in the space of five rounds.

After the second interval all the rounds were tied, except for the conundrum: John deduced that 'ALONGCOAT' was 'octagonal', to make the final score of 117-87 look more respectable. I wasn't surprised that Paul won - but everyone, including Paul, was taken aback by the margin of victory.

It was well into the evening when the recording finished. I had hoped to see the semi-final of the European Cup, in which Arsenal were competing (Sue and her sons are big fans, and I always support English teams when they play in Europe). As it was I only caught the last quarter of an hour, including the penalty save which ensured Arsenal's passage to the final. It was a thrilling end to a memorable day. When I returned to the hotel room, I called Sue and my parents to fill them in on the story of the day, and browsed some word lists before bedtime.

The second day's filming involved an earlier start than the first. We assembled in a crowded Green Room. The television was on in readiness for the first show, and while we waited for the first two contestants to be called through we watched - with great hilarity - a double bill of Pingu! I had never seen the programme before, but was amused by the subtle humour which underlay the penguin's antics. The episode in which Pingu was splattered from above by a seagull made us all chuckle. The fact that we had found a children's programme so entertaining became something of a standing joke among the backstage regulars.

The competition resumed with the sixth first-round match, between series 53 beaten finalist John Brackstone and the beaten finalist from series 49, David Wilson. Prior to the show, we saw some examples of David's work (in postcard form) exhibited on the screen: pictures of ducks, and very impressive they were.

Several early rounds went John's way: 'elixirs' and 'deviants' were winners, and when David risked '*billeter*' to no avail John went 21 points ahead with 'belter'. Although David pulled back slightly in the first numbers game, John pressed on after the interval, extending his lead with 'reputes' and 'insofar'. In an attempt to get back in the game, David opted for 'four from the top' for his first choice of numbers; however, it was John who hit the target, making the scores 64:31 in his favour as the second part of the show drew to a close.

The game was as good as over when John spotted 'wrenches' in round eleven. Another winning word ('fonder') came in round thirteen, before David reduced the deficit in the final numbers game. He had again requested all the large numbers, to Carol's dismay - although she was the only one to get the target spot on!

The conundrum was tricky: SNOWFABLE eluded both contestants. Backstage we were all flummoxed until about halfway through the thirty seconds, when suddenly Matt and I worked out at the same time that the solution was 'wolfsbane'. I was aware that Matt would be my opponent in the quarter-final if he won his forthcoming game against Chris Cummins, and thought that if it came to a crucial conundrum between us it was likely to be close!

John's final total was 86, to David's 48. Afterwards David expressed his disappointment with the quality of his final performance on Countdown; but he was a true sportsman and made a very dignified exit.

The next game would give an indication of Paul Gallen's form, as he took on series 50 finalist Eamonn Timmins. It turned out to be a much higher scoring game than the previous match. In the second letters game Eamonn took a six-point lead, after Paul - uncharacteristically - missed a fairly easy word, 'fences'. This seemed to spur Paul into action. In the very next round he came up with a nine-letter word, 'resonated', to take a twelve-point advantage, which he extended in round six with 'stoical'. Another nine-letter word, 'reshaping', soon followed. Eamonn's failure to spot it all but put an end to the contest, and it became a question of how many points Paul might amass.

Some good eight-letter words and a straightforward numbers game saw a century on the board for the young Irishman after just eleven rounds. Eamonn was keeping pace with him at this point, and managed to do so for the rest of the game. 'Dioramas', 'festoon' and another undemanding numbers game took Paul up to 125. If he could solve the conundrum, he would post an entry high on the list of Countdown's all-time top scores.

It turned out to be a particularly difficult conundrum: HUESTREET, with its three 'e's, didn't seem to bear any relationship to anything. The thirty seconds soon expired, leaving Paul disappointed, and Eamonn bidding farewell.

In the Green Room we were all doing our best to solve the conundrum: after about twenty seconds I noticed the possible ending '-ette'. This quickly led me to the answer, 'usherette'. I was feeling confident that I was in peak form at this point: I had seen 'resonated' and 'reshaping' as well, and I couldn't recall missing anything in this game. I knew it would take three more performances of that calibre to win the championship, and I would need to produce one of them shortly, against the winner of the next game.

It was just as the curtain went down on the contest between Paul and Eamonn that Sue arrived at the studio. I was glad that she was going to have at least one opportunity to watch a show in which I was involved. We were in the canteen when Chris Cummins, who had arrived that morning unaccompanied, came in, so we asked him to join us. It turned out that Chris had also written a novel, so we had an interesting discussion about our literary experiences.

The match between Chris and Matt looked sure to be enthralling. I knew Matt was in great form; on the other hand

Chris, whose triumph had occurred over two years ago, seemed to think he would be a bit rusty. All his eleven victories in series 50 had been comfortable. I certainly would have been struggling to match him, although this was before I had begun concentrating on developing my skills at Countdown.

The game began with a couple of tied rounds, before Matt went ahead when his 'inrushes' beat Chris's 'inshore'. However, they both missed the nine-letter word 'nourishes', to the surprise of those assembled in the Green Room. There followed one of the longest ever sequences of rounds in which the points were shared. Six times they came up with the same word: 'spatted', 'hoofers', 'balletic', 'oddments', 'punter' and 'clamped', and two other letters games were tied with different words. Both contestants came up with solutions to the numbers games at the end of the first part of the show, and again at the end of the second part. In all there were ten consecutive tied rounds, with the result that as the last numbers were being selected Matt led by 99 points to 91. Just as he had done many times in series 50 Chris asked for 'six small numbers'. 577 proved a challenging target. Chris had clearly finished before the thirty seconds had elapsed. However, Matt remained deep in concentration. The disappointment in Matt's voice was clear, as he declared that he had only managed 579. Chris's calculations were spot on, giving him a slender advantage with just one round remaining.

If anyone had asked me at the start of the previous day how many of the eight games in the first round would be decided by crucial conundrums, I would have guessed at three or four. It had taken until the final first round game for it to happen. I waited with bated breath to see which of these two outstanding players I would face. Des pressed the button and RUMPIZETA appeared on the monitor. One second was all that was needed before a buzzer sounded. Matt's light shone forth. With a look of great relief he revealed that the answer was 'trapezium'. Chris applauded his opponent's speed of thought, and accepted his misfortune with good grace.

Chapter 14: 'One of the best games ever!'

At last I knew who my quarter-final opponent would be. I got the impression that Matt was still feeling the elation of victory: he approached our show in such a buoyant mood that it was almost contagious. Of all the people I competed with on the show, Matt was the least affected by the tension, and the most able to be himself in the spotlight. In the preamble to the show, Des mimicked Tom Jones, pulling the Welshman's leg about his moustache. Matt echoed this by starting to make his first letters selection with a Welsh accent. When my turn followed, I felt compelled to extend the humorous episode by doing likewise, even though I'm not particularly good at impressions.

In the first round Matt's choice of letters didn't look too promising, and we struggled to find six-letter words; Matt had 'loaner', while I had 'trowel'.

Things looked up in the second round, when we each saw sevens; mine was 'adoptee', whereas Matt risked 'outdate'. Curiously enough I had recently checked Matt's word, as I had spotted it in a practice game, and had discovered it as a derivative of 'outdated'. Matt got the points he was due and the scores moved on to 13:13.

The next two letters rounds set the pattern for most of the rest of the game, in that we shared the points with identical words. 'Munches' stood out in round three, while in round four 'ladders' was the best we could manage.

It was Matt's choice of numbers, and he opted for three large and three small ones. The target came out at 335, and there was a 5 among the small numbers. I obtained the 67 needed to complete the equation by subtracting 8 from 75. It seemed to fall into place quite readily, and I didn't expect to win the round - but Matt declared 337. Des wanted to know how I had managed to spot this method, so Carol explained the thinking behind my solution, describing it as 'neat'.

The scores moved on to 37:27 as the first interval approached.

In Dictionary Corner Ann Widdecombe then showed that she could enjoy a laugh at her own expense. She told the story of how she had been heckled throughout a talk she had given to the British Medical Association, only to be told by the organisers that it was the first time in years that the person concerned had said anything sensible!

After the break we took up where we had left off with the letters games, adding seven points to our respective totals with 'concise', which I saw just before the thirty seconds expired.

The next round provided the sort of moment you dream about - when a nine-letter word falls into place as soon as all the letters are on the board. I spent the whole of the thirty seconds looking as though I was deep in thought, so as not to give the game away. I knew that if it proved to be a winner I would have a commanding lead. But Matt had spotted 'paintiest' too. Des was intrigued to know whether we had been sure that it was a valid word. I confirmed that I was certain of it, while Matt, who had seemed a little doubtful, declared in a tongue-in-cheek manner that it was a word he used every day. Des remarked that he wouldn't be coming round to visit Matt's house!

In round eight I spotted 'overrun' with just enough time remaining for me to scribble it down. It was becoming so predictable that we would come up with the same word that Matt simply passed his sheet of paper over to Ann and joked that he didn't even have to say it!

Des complimented us on our scores, which now stood at 69:59. There followed another round where we came up with an identical word - this time it was 'quieten'. It then fell to me to choose some numbers. I opted for 'four from the top row', hoping to reap the benefits of all the practice I had done with this combination. When the two small numbers turned out to be 4 and 4, Carol groaned! But a target of 187 seemed achievable. I saw a method of obtaining this figure fairly early on and wrote it down. As there was time to check it, I reworked the calculation, and it came out differently. There was no time to resolve the discrepancy, so I declared 187 rather uncertainly, in the hope that my original calculations were right. As I went through them with Carol I was relieved to find that they were indeed correct. Matt had arrived at the target by another method, and yet another round was tied. The scores at the second interval stood at 86:76. Surely we would both go on to make centuries?

When we resumed with Matt's choice of letters another promising selection emerged. Once 'hairnets' fell into place from the first eight letters, I hoped that Matt would choose a vowel: an 'o' was all that was required for 'hortensia', while an 'e' would generate 'herniates'. Matt did indeed go for a vowel, and an 'e' came out! So for the second time in the game I kept my head down and looked as though I was still at work. Once again, however, Matt had spotted the same word, which he wisely chose to declare in preference to the speculative *'antherise'*. The scores now stood at 104:94 in my favour.

In round 12 I was presented with a dilemma. Matt declared a seven. I had seen 'gustier' and could have settled for a share of the points. However, I had come up with a risky eight, *'pursiest'*. I knew that 'pursiness' was a word, and deduced that there must be an adjective 'pursy'. I had a vague recollection that I had come across the superlative before, but I knew that since 'pursy' was a two-syllable adjective, *'pursiest'* would have to be specified in the dictionary in order for it to be allowable. Given that my lead remained at ten points, I was aware that as things stood Matt would be able to level the scores by spotting the conundrum, so forcing an extra conundrum. So I decided to seize the opportunity to extend my advantage to eighteen points with three rounds to play - an altogether more comfortable position. Susie checked the dictionary under 'pursy' (out of breath), but the superlative was not specified.

Ironically, as Paul Howe pointed out to me later, I could have had a safe eight, by using the same letters to make 'pisteurs' (a term for those in charge of a piste).

Matt claimed seven points with 'sprites' to notch up his century. But at least I still led by three points. In the next round, the first seven letters suggested the possibility that 'folkloric' might fall into place. Could there be a third nine-letter word in this already remarkable game?

It was not to be. Indeed the last two letters ensured instead that a challenging problem confronted us. I struggled to a risky five: I recalled having seen the word '*flook*' somewhere, although I had no idea where, or what it meant. It turned out that it wasn't in the dictionary. Some weeks later I happened upon a pop group called 'Flook' while browsing in a music store; but I still don't think this was where I had come across the word, as I subsequently recalled that the creators of the Spitting Image puppets were called Flook and Law. I probably spent too many of the thirty seconds contemplating '*flook*', as I not only missed a safe five, 'aloof', but also failed to notice the six that secured the points for Matt, namely 'formal'. Susie drew our attention to a word which had somehow slipped through the net during my trawls through the dictionary - 'aliform' (wing-shaped).

Matt had taken the lead for the first time in the match. With just two rounds remaining, I couldn't win before the conundrum – however, I could lose if I didn't score in the numbers game. I opted for 'three from the top', perhaps influenced by the outcome of the first numbers game. 255 proved an easy target for both of us.

The drama of the crucial conundrum was certain to follow, but it was preceded by a moment of humour. After I had explained my calculations to Carol, Matt passed his piece of paper my way, instead of giving it to Ann to check. I assumed he wanted to show it to Des, so I passed it on. When Des queried this, Matt explained that he wanted *me* to look at it, so Des passed it back. I checked it briefly, then heartily congratulated Matt for getting it 'spot on'. Des joked that I should have changed a number to make it wrong!

Our scores moved on to 117:114. Des had the statistics concerning the programme's history to hand, and he observed that, regardless of what happened with the conundrum, the losing score would be the highest ever!

And so we bowed our heads, prepared to press our buzzers, and focused on our monitors. When 'SILLYQUOO' appeared, my finger seemed to react faster than my mind! It might as well have said 'soliloquy'! Momentarily I thought I might have jumped to the wrong conclusion, but by the time Des asked me for my declaration I was certain. The scores changed for the final time to 124:117.

Matt had seen 'soliloquy' too, and had depressed his buzzer a fraction of a second too late. Of course, I was pleased that I was going through to the semi-final, but I really felt for him, not only for having reached so high a score without winning, but also to have missed out so narrowly on the conundrum. When Des confirmed that Matt had set a record score for a defeated contestant, Matt commented ruefully that he would be remembered as a loser. I commented that Matt was 'definitely not a loser'. I knew how close I had come to being the one knocked out.

Afterwards Des asked me whether I thought I could go on and win the series. 'I hope so', I replied. I wouldn't have dared to be more positive than that. I knew that I would have to come through two really tough matches to reach that goal.

A photo-shoot followed, involving all the contestants plus Carol, Des, Susie and Ann. It was quite an exercise in logistics to get us all in the frame, and there were some very ungainly poses! Afterwards, as I was making my way back to the Green Room, I came across Steve Graston. He and Michelle were clutching two large sheets of card. I learned that these had been removed from the numbers board after Carol had used them to record our calculations the previous day. Steve very kindly gave me one of these sheets. We then went back into the studio, where Carol was waiting to sign autographs. I collected one from her on behalf of a colleague at work, and then asked if she would sign the sheet of card which Steve had given me. When Carol took the card, I expected her to simply put her name on it. Instead she wrote: '*Mark, you're an absolute star. Thank you so much for making these finals so extraordinary. Lots of love, Carol V. xx*'. I need hardly say that this was a really proud moment for me.

There was one more show to be recorded that day. It promised to be another thriller: Paul Gallen was to take on John Davies. Des commented at the start that he thought the standard of the previous show would be maintained. As if to reinforce this statement, both players declared a nine in the first round. Paul's 'stingaree' was excellent, but John was not so lucky with '*gratinees*', as the word 'gratinee' is only listed as an adjective.

Thereafter most of the rounds were tied with maximum scores. Paul missed 'cabbie', enabling John to reduce the deficit to twelve points. John tried valiantly to use his arithmetical prowess to his advantage. First he tried a selection of six small numbers, which resulted in the points being shared. Later, in the penultimate round, he went for 'four large numbers'. Although the target of 314 was in fact achievable, both players declared that they were one away.

Paul gave an explanation of his calculations, and they were correct. He had preserved his twelve-point lead and had avoided a crucial conundrum.

Paul's face, indeed his whole torso, exuded relief. Given that his only other really close match had been our series 52 final, it's not surprising that he should have been so glad to pull through on this occasion. Paul capped his performance by spotting the conundrum, 'godfather', almost immediately, to bring the final scores to 118:96. John put a brave face on the matter and acknowledged that he had known that Paul was capable of winning.

Chapter 15: 'So far, so good'

Sixteen possible winners had been whittled down to six over the two days. Only Conor and I remained unbeaten. I realised that the standard was such that there would almost inevitably be more crucial conundrums the next day. So after we had finished our meal in the hotel that evening I looked through the list of likely conundrums I had compiled, numbering around a thousand. Sue helped me by reading some out for me to solve, omitting those where she was unable to read my writing! I was able to give the answers to the majority within a couple of seconds.

A good night's sleep was essential, and happily I managed to achieve this, despite the buzz of excitement I was still feeling as a result of the day's events, combined with a certain amount of apprehension over what would happen the following day.

When we arrived at the studio the next morning we gathered in the Green Room and again amused ourselves by watching a couple of episodes of Pingu. Although they weren't quite as funny as the episode featuring the seagull which we had seen the previous day, they served to lighten the atmosphere in the run-up to the 'serious' business that would follow.

Conor and John Brackstone's quarter-final would launch the proceedings. Shortly before recording was due to begin, Sharon came in to the Green Room and asked whether those of us who had chosen to stay there would mind joining the audience, as there weren't that many people in the studio that morning. We agreed, albeit reluctantly, as we were used to the comfort and freedom of the Green Room. Sue and I sat alongside Paul Gallen and his dad Philip in an empty row at the back of the audience.

We had noticed that Conor seemed really tired that morning. The recordings of the finals of series 54 had taken place the previous week, and Conor was now well into his second week of playing Countdown against top opponents. It soon became apparent that he wasn't at his best. In the second round he went seven points behind as a result of missing 'festoon'. Both players spotted the nine-letter word 'esplanade' in round three, following it up with some none too obvious sevens in round four. But John was able to extend his lead after Conor realised he had made a mistake in the first numbers game. Des noted the uniqueness of the situation: Conor was fourteen points adrift.

After the break Conor reduced the deficit to seven points with 'minored.' Three successive tied rounds followed, before Conor was able to take the lead after John missed a relatively straightforward target in the second numbers game. Any suggestion that Conor was out of the woods was short-lived: in round twelve his six-letter word, 'sourly', was surpassed by a seven from John, in the form of 'sorrily', taking the scores to 80:76 in John's favour.

Three rounds remained. In the last letters game Conor came up with what Susie described as his 'best word yet': 'bresaola' (an Italian dish). So the lead changed hands for the third time, and now it was Conor who was four points ahead. A tricky numbers game added to the tension: neither contestant managed to get 688 spot on. John had 680, but Conor was closer, with 683. Getting within five of the target earned him seven points. Conor's lead extended to eleven, with just the conundrum remaining. With the game safe, Conor rounded it off by working out that 'KEVINBARR' was actually 'riverbank', taking the final score to 101:80. John accepted defeat with characteristic dignity and generously conceded that Conor deserved to win.

We returned to the Green Room, and congratulated both players on their performance. When Sharon came in to ask if we would go back into the audience, we declined apologetically. Personally I found that being backstage was far more conducive to feeling relaxed and comfortable. With my semi-final and potentially the final to come, I was determined to avoid doing anything which might detract from my performance and jeopardise my chances of winning.

The next game would determine who my semi-final opponent would be. It promised to be a tight contest between Paul Howe and Jack. Victory for the latter would set up a repeat of our series 52 semi-final. Irrespective of the outcome of this contest, a repeat of the final itself was distinctly possible.

After the first round was shared with seven-letter words, Paul took a six-point lead when Jack had *'choruser'* disallowed. A couple of shared rounds followed before Jack suffered further misfortune in the first numbers game, when he was unable to recall his calculations. In round seven Paul produced a winning eight, 'burgonet', so amassing a commanding lead of twenty-one points. But Jack struck back in the second numbers game, hitting the bull's-eye to reduce the deficit to eleven points.

After the break the remaining letters games were all tied. For the final numbers game, Paul asked for 'one from the top, and five small numbers'. Carol, recognising that this was a tactic for defending a lead, commented with a smile that he didn't want to take any chances!

Paul's shrewdness was rewarded when 481 proved quite achievable for both contestants. An irrelevant conundrum foxed both Paul and Jack: Carol remarked that 'IRISHCORS' (cirrhosis) was one of the hardest conundrums she had seen in years. The final score was 83:72. Paul obviously wasn't over-impressed by the standard of his performance in this game, despite his victory. He joked to me afterwards that he felt sure it would have left me quaking in my boots! Although I had spotted a couple of things both players had missed, and had solved the conundrum after about fifteen seconds, I would definitely have lost a couple of rounds. I hadn't been keeping score, and certainly wasn't convinced that I would have won that game.

At lunchtime I discussed the morning's games with Sue and we agreed that the standard had gone down. We attributed this to fatigue setting in. I assured Sue that I felt fine. 'Well, you are nocturnal!' she replied. We were seated in the canteen when we saw Jack come in. We called him and asked if he wanted to join us. I remember saying that we would understand if he preferred to be on his own, as I wondered whether he might want to spend some time quietly getting over his disappointment at being knocked out. But Jack was glad to join us, and was clearly not too upset about his defeat. We had time to have a good chat before returning to the Green Room.

My semi-final contest with Paul was next on the schedule. I had won the toss and opted for the challenger's chair.

Paul's choice of letters yielded a favourite Countdown word: 'wagoner'. It was a word for which I had devised an imaginative technique for remembering its alternative spelling: just as you can have one or two horses (gee-gees) pulling the vehicle, so you can have one or two 'gees' in 'wagon' or 'wagoner'. I was therefore not in any doubt that it was correctly spelt. Paul declared a seven too, but even as he began to say 'carnage' he realised that there was only one 'a' in the selection.

I had the lead straight away, but it didn't last long: in the next round my seven-letter word, 'entices', was beaten by an excellent eight from Paul, 'niceties'. A difficult set of letters followed, from which we both managed sixes: Paul spotted 'hoarse', while I saw 'haloes'. Again the work I had done on alternative spellings came in useful: I was aware that 'haloes' could be spelt with or without the 'e'.

In the next round my choice of letters also provided nothing better than sixes. Out of a number of possibilities, we both went for 'elated', bringing our scores to 19:18 in Paul's favour.

When Paul selected 'four from the top', and the two small numbers came out as 6 and 10, the target of 954 looked distinctly hittable. I tried to find 6×159, but couldn't create the 9 I needed to add to $100 + 50$.

I looked instead for $(10 \times 96) - 6$. However, 96 is not a number which can be created from the four large numbers alone. In the end both Paul and I arrived at 953 and were awarded 7 points each. I managed to find this solution during the interval: $(100 + 6) \times 9$, with the nine being manufactured as follows: $10 - (\{75-25\}/50)$. Although I was annoyed with myself for not spotting it sooner, I knew there was no point in giving it any further thought, so I shrugged it off and got on with the game.

Our scores stood at 26:25. Des transposed them when he gave them out, mistakenly crediting me with the lead. I joked with Paul, who had been very much part of the behind-the-scenes camaraderie, that we could swap if he liked. Someone among the crew noticed Des's error and there was a retake.

There followed a scene in which Des's sense of humour came to the fore. Kim Woodman delved around under Des's desk and pulled out various items of clutter: a teddy bear, a model of Des, which had been made by a viewer, and a miniature skeleton. When Kim described the skeleton as an ex-girlfriend Des corrected her by saying that it was actually a current girlfriend! Kim went on to produce a handbag, whereupon Des observed 'Don't knock it until you've tried it!' - a comment he repeated when Kim came across a bra!

All this proved to be a prelude to Kim's explanation of how the researchers for her programme go about selecting houses which are dirty enough to warrant a complete overhaul. Apparently those households that are grubby enough have one thing in common: they haven't entertained any visitors for at least ten years!

As a result of this lengthy entertainment the gap between rounds five and six seemed unusually long. This didn't seem to affect the concentration levels of either of us, as when we resumed we both came up with sevens from a difficult five-vowel selection: Paul had 'mermaid', while I spotted 'diorama'.

In the next round Paul's choice of letters yielded a promising looking bunch. However, I spent most of the thirty seconds stuck on a seven-letter word, 'listens'. Finally it occurred to me to add the 'g' on the front to make 'glistens'. It was just as well I saw this, as Paul had used the same letters to make 'singlets'. Susie then revealed that there was in fact a nine, albeit one of which she didn't approve. This must have triggered a reaction in my mind, because I then realised what the word was: 'losingest', an American word which I also thought too slangy to warrant inclusion in the dictionary. For the second time in the game, I felt really disappointed to have missed an opportunity. I was still a point behind, when I could so easily have been comfortably ahead.

We moved on to another tricky five-vowel selection - my fault again! From this we managed nothing better than five-letter words: Paul saw 'erode', while I had 'ready'. The letters in the next round didn't look particularly promising. Paul came up with a six letter word, 'uplift', and I thought I had matched his effort with *'talipo'*. However, Susie clarified that it was necessary to add a 't' on the end for 'talipot' (an Indian palm). So Paul extended his lead to seven points.

My choice of numbers followed. I went for 'three large numbers', hoping for a challenging target. However, 240 proved no problem for either of us. As the second interval approached the scores stood at 63:56. An exciting finish was surely on the cards.

We resumed with yet another five-vowel selection, this time at Paul's behest. The letters were much more promising this time: Paul produced an eight with 'diagnose', and I used the same eight letters to make 'agonised'. Round twelve was also tied, this time with sevens. Paul came up with 'hideous', while I saw 'duchies' - a word which appeared on the list of unfamiliar words which I had prepared just before the tournament. It was the only entry on the list which I used in any of my games - but it had come at a really important time, so much so that it was justification in itself for the hours I had spent on this task.

With three rounds to play, the gap remained at seven points, and there was still everything to play for. A promising looking selection of letters appeared: I quickly spotted the eight-letter word 'atomiser', and spent the rest of the thirty seconds trying to find a way of using the leftover 'f' to make a nine. I was fairly sure that I would have recognised the combination if it had yielded a nine, and was therefore satisfied that there wasn't one.

After I declared my eight, Paul hesitated, and then decided to risk a nine. It was a bold move. If it paid off his lead would be 25 with two rounds remaining, and the game would be over. He came up with '*formatise*'. It was a very plausible word, but it didn't sound familiar to me, in the way I would have expected it to if it were in the dictionary. Susie had the book open at the right page, but this was because she had spotted 'formates'. A quick examination confirmed that Paul's effort was indeed invalid. I regained the lead that I had last held at the end of round one, this time by a single point.

My choice of numbers followed. Realising that I could now clinch the match before the conundrum, but that I couldn't lose it before that, I chose 'six small ones' - in my opinion the most difficult numbers selection. It was the only time I had ever gone for this combination. But it was a logical choice, as it meant that it was almost certain to be a challenge, as well as a test of nerve - the sort of situation I had thrived on so far.

When the target came out at 256 it looked achievable: I knew that this number fitted into the sequence formed by multiplying 2 by itself, and there were two 2s, as well as an 8 in the selection. I fairly quickly came up with a means of making 8×32, and even had time to write it down neatly. Paul proved equal to the challenge: he came up with a similar method of arriving at 256, and our scores moved on to 89:88 in my favour.

So once again I faced a crucial conundrum. By now it was all becoming part of the routine, and I had got past feeling nervous. None of Paul's previous games had got to this stage, so I had an advantage in that respect. Although I knew that if neither of us solved the conundrum I would win by a point, this could not have been further from my mind as I moved my finger onto the buzzer and bowed my head over the monitor.

Whereas in the quarter-final 'soliloquy' had sprung to mind and I hadn't had to think at all, when 'STUARTFIR' appeared on the monitor I knew I was going to have to work on it, although it did strike me almost immediately that it looked like a combination of two words. Suddenly I saw 'fruit', and it was a short step from there to seeing 'starfruit'. After six seconds had elapsed I was able to press the buzzer and experience the relief of knowing that I had scraped through in yet another close encounter!

Paul modestly said that he hadn't expected to get that far. It had come as no surprise to me, though, as I had considered him a possible winner of the tournament even before it started. Paul was very sporting and later wished me luck in the final.

Des pointed out that I was now unbeaten in fourteen appearances on Countdown. I nodded and replied 'So far, so good'. It was a reflection of my awareness that I had ridden my luck yet again, and that I was going to need to do so one more time if I was to remain unbeaten. In an extension of our conversation, which didn't make it into the televised version of the show, Des asked me whether I was aware of what lay ahead in the final. 'Yes,' I replied, 'two awesome opponents!'

In reality, at this point I was feeling jubilant. I had set myself two objectives from the start: one, of course, was to win the series and become 'Champion of Champions'. The other was to do well enough to generate the rest of the material required to write the book you are now reading. To be sure of achieving this, I had to be involved in the climax to the series. It wouldn't have made a particularly good ending if I had written about the final from the point of view of a spectator, rather than a participant. Win or lose, I was going to have cause for celebration!

It was time to find out which of the 'two awesome opponents' I would face. We took our places in the Green Room. I had made up my mind not to try to 'play along' with this game. Of course, after years of joining in it was second nature to look and see what might be possible. However, I didn't concentrate in the way I would if I were actually involved, or if I were watching at home. The reason was that I didn't want to do anything that might have a negative impact on the 'comfort zone' into which I had settled. I was feeling confident, to the point where it wouldn't have made any difference if I had 'won' this semi-final. On the other hand, if I were to find that I would have struggled, it might have undermined my positivism. So I took on the role of an interested observer. The quality of the performance I was about to witness left me in no doubt that I was going to have to be at my absolute best to have any chance in the final.

When Des introduced the contestants, he commented that it was going to be a nerve-wracking afternoon for the two boys. Paul, now aged twenty, looked every bit as nervous as he had before our series final, and Conor, aged just fourteen, looked less comfortable than usual. There is no doubt in my mind that being in my forties - older than the other two contestants put together - was a distinct advantage in this respect. But would I be able to make it count?

Des remarked on Conor's record of thirteen consecutive wins, adding: 'He's never been beaten. Could this be the day? We'll find out.'

The first letters selection looked really tricky, the sort of combination that would often produce nothing more than five-letter words in a normal game. Both players made it look easy, spotting 'adaptors' for eight points.

There was an amusing moment after the second letters game. When Paul produced 'mourned', Conor matched it with 'minored'. This prompted Des to comment that the latter word had come up recently. Conor nodded diplomatically. Only when Des asked him whether he had been watching, did Conor reveal that in fact he was the person who had offered it! Des's reply was to assert that 'he'll be taking the show over soon!'

The deadlock prevailed in the third round, in which both contestants spotted 'smearier' for eight points. But in round four there was an uncharacteristic lapse by Conor, who missed both 'moping', which Paul declared, and 'pigeon', although he did have an entertaining five in 'boing'. Paul's choice of 'three large numbers' produced an easy target of 749, with the result that the scores at the end of the first part were 39:33 in Paul's favour.

In round six both contestants spotted 'tumble'. The next letters game produced an extraordinary moment. Conor offered 'ritenuto', leaving Des looking bewildered, and when Paul declared the same word, it became apparent that everybody, including Susie, was dumbfounded. 'I'm learning so much', Susie commented humbly, after she had looked the word up and explained that it was a musical term for a reduction in tempo.

Thereafter the points were shared time and time again: 'pointed' stood out in round eight; then both contestants saw 'rerated' in round nine. 321 proved no problem for either contestant in the second numbers game. The scores reached 77:71 at the end of the second part of the programme. I was still none the wiser as to who my opponent was going to be.

Some excellent words emerged in round eleven: Conor saw 'holiness', while Paul continued the musical theme with 'helicons' (a form of tuba). At this point Paul had taken maximum points in every round. But in the letters game that followed he actually missed something: 'ketosis' was the one that got away. Paul was clearly miffed that he had let slip an opportunity to put some distance between his score and Conor's, acknowledging that it was a word of which he had heard. As it was both players saw 'tossed', and the gap remained at six points.

The final letters game produced yet another tie, as both contestants saw 'organic'. Could the last numbers game resolve the issue? Conor, knowing he could not afford to lose it, chose 'one large number and five small ones'. He had said earlier that he thought the numbers games were not his strongest point, and he was presumably hoping to get an easy target, with a view to using his monumental conundrum-solving skills to pip Paul at the post. Conor got his wish: 806 was indeed an easy target, and both players finished their calculations with time to spare.

The scores moved on to 108:102. Remarkably, both players had reached their centuries without there being a nine-letter word in the game. In the Green Room, all eyes were glued to the screen as we waited for the crucial conundrum to be revealed. From the time when I had first seen the draw for the tournament, I had envisaged that if I made it to the final I would be most likely to face Conor. But I also knew that Paul was someone who *could* topple Conor, and felt that his form in the series so far would have made him a slight favourite at the start of the game. Now it was all down to the lottery of a crucial conundrum . . .

'CHOPLOSER' appeared on the monitor: in an instant the light came on below Paul's desk. Backstage, I muttered the answer to myself as Paul correctly stated: 'preschool'.

Instantly I felt really sorry for Conor. He had played so well, and had raised his game to meet the challenge that Paul's outstanding performance had presented him with. The conundrum itself had an unfortunate pertinence about it. The loser was indeed for the chop, and Conor certainly didn't deserve to lose, any more than Paul did. When Des asked him how he felt about experiencing defeat, Conor answered that he was 'relieved'. It wasn't hard to understand why he should have felt this way: it was a tall order for anyone of his age, however talented, to continue taking on older people and beating them.

When he returned to the Green Room, Conor displayed remarkable resilience and maturity. He simply shook his head and said he didn't care about his defeat. I remember speaking to his father later and saying that he must feel very proud of him. Mr Travers had an exemplary attitude: he seemed to take everything in his stride, and was very supportive of his son, without creating any pressure by way of expectation.

Chapter 16: A conundrum too far!

During the time which remained before the final Sue and I stayed in the Green Room, and chatted with the other contestants. A number of them had asked to buy copies of 'A Nightmare in *Paradise*', so I distributed these, and signed them. Inevitably, the thought of the forthcoming contest was uppermost in my mind. At some point it occurred to me that if anyone was going to make it to the end of the series with their unbeaten record intact, it had to be me; Conor's exit had left me as the only unbeaten contestant. I felt quite proud that I was the 'last man standing' in that respect.

When I saw Philip Gallen I smiled and said: 'Here we are again!'

'Yes,' he replied, 'but we're going to have to turn things around this time, Mark!'

Sharon came in to attend to the toss of the coin, which would determine who sat where. Paul called 'heads', but it was 'tails'. It was a foregone conclusion that I would choose the challenger's chair, thereby putting myself in a position to make the vital third numbers selection in the penultimate round. I feel sure Paul would have preferred the challenger's seat. He looked rather disgruntled at the outcome as he headed back towards where he had been standing with his father.

When the time came to go through to the studio Sue gave me an instruction.

'You must win!' she said.

'Okay', I replied, 'I'll make sure I do that!'

It was a great feeling, turning from the corridor into the studio for the fifteenth and last time to take part in the final of the Champion of Champions series. I might have *hoped* when it all began some eighteen months before that it would all end in this arena, perhaps even have *believed* that it would, but I certainly couldn't have counted on it!

When Des came in I chatted with him, and told him that I would like to say thank you to everyone at the end. He asked me whether I wanted to do this regardless of whether I won or lost, and I affirmed that it made no difference. He also asked whether I was doing any writing at the moment. I explained that I had put my novelistic activities on hold until after the series had been filmed, and that I now intended to write about my experiences on Countdown, which he agreed was a good idea. I also mentioned that I had a conundrum for him, but I didn't reveal that it was 'DESINGOAL' at that point, just in case it happened to be the one to be used in the show! I reasoned that if Damian had set about making up football oriented conundrums in the way that I had hoped, he might well have come up with 'DESINGOAL' and decided to amuse everyone with it in the final programme. If this were so, it would be awkward for Des, who would have known what the conundrum was, if I had begun discussing it with him at that point! So I explained that I would tell him what it was after the final had finished.

When the time came for the recording to start I felt surprisingly calm. Looking back, I would attribute this to several factors. One was that, as the number of episodes in which I was involved grew, it became more and more possible to view the whole thing as routine. Also, the closer I came to achieving my goal, the easier I felt it would be to accept the disappointment if I didn't make it. In particular, my presence in the final meant that I would not have to endure the experience of watching a game in which I had dreamed of taking part. When the famous Countdown theme tune was played to introduce the contest, just as it is when the show is transmitted, I even felt relaxed enough to hum along!

When the time came for the contestants to be introduced,

Des began by mentioning once again that I was a writer and driver 'from Hove actually'. He then went on to say that in fourteen appearances on Countdown, I had never been vanquished. It was the proudest moment of all for me. I felt then that irrespective of the result of the final I had achieved something remarkable.

Someone among the staff had pointed out to Des that this was a rematch, but had obviously not gone into detail regarding the series 52 final. During the preamble to the show Des asked more about the original contest. He wanted to know whether I could remember what the crucial conundrum had been. How could I ever forget, I thought to myself, as I uttered the word 'partridge'? An extension of Des's enquiry, which was edited from the televised version of the show, saw him ask Paul whether he had been close to spotting the conundrum. Paul was clearly reluctant to elaborate on this matter, and suggested to Des that he watch it on the video. Soon after this, everyone's thoughts turned to speculation on who was going to be crowned 'Champion of Champions'.

As Paul had been assigned to the champion's chair, the contest began with his choice of letters. It looked a tricky selection. For most of the thirty seconds I couldn't do better than a six. With moments to spare I spotted the ending '-fish', and then realised it was possible to make 'starfish'. I didn't have time to write the word down, and had only just satisfied myself that it was indeed there when Des asked for my declaration. Paul had the same word and we shared the points.

Round two was my choice of letters. Again, it didn't look too promising, but I managed to spot 'sunbeam'. I was hopeful this might be a winner, but Paul had seen it too. It was 15:15.

From Paul's next choice of letters the word 'noodles' stood out, and it also looked obvious that there was nothing better. Seven points were added to each of our totals.

Round four was my choice of letters. The comparative 'runtier' fell into place as the letters came out, and thirty seconds of contemplation yielded nothing better. My hopes that Paul might not have known this rather bizarre word proved unfounded.

After four rounds we had accumulated 29 points from identical words. Paul chose 'three from the top' - a favourite combination of mine, and one that had secured a critical ten points for me in our series 52 final. I inferred from his choice that he had been practising with this combination since then! The target of 620 proved no trouble for either of us, although we did at least manage to come up with different solutions, which Carol said were among a number of ways of reaching the target.

We were then entertained by Kim Woodman, who gave us two short anecdotes, one about the origin of the four-poster bed, the other about an amusing encounter she had had with a disgruntled Liverpudlian lady.

During the break I went to say something to Paul - I forget what. I quickly realised that he was deep in concentration and was clearly intent on remaining that way. During the second interval a whole conversation, initiated by Susie about a crossword clue which had left her stumped, took place around Paul without there being any indication that he was aware it was happening!

When we resumed on 39 points apiece it was my choice of letters. The first eight letters to appear yielded 'cellaret'. I wasn't sure of the meaning, but I was fairly sure it was a word, so I asked for a final consonant in the hope that it would be an 's'. Instead an 'r' came out. Another thirty seconds of fruitless deliberation was followed by another round where we scored the same number of points with the same word. It was 47:47.

From Paul's choice of letters the word 'montage' stood out, but there was nothing better. Paul used the same seven letters to make 'magneto'. Round eight provided us with an easy eight-letter word, 'remained', while 'refuting' seemed to stand out a mile in round nine, as did the fact that the leftover 'f' was useless - although I kept on trying to deploy it right up to the end of the thirty seconds.

The score stood at seventy points each. I now had my first choice of numbers. I asked for 'four from the top', hoping for a challenging target which might enable me to break the deadlock. My plan was thwarted when a target figure of 175 appeared. Although the thirty seconds were superfluous, Des set the clock in motion as is customary in such situations. We had raced to eighty points each, and neither of us had missed any opportunity to outdo the other.

At the start of the final I would have said that a crucial conundrum was very likely. At this point it seemed inevitable. As we waited to resume our enthralling contest I went back over the dozen or so conundrums that I had singled out as possibly the most appropriate choices for a Champion of Champions final, including STARTITLE -

rattliest, SEESTITLE - steeliest, CREAMYPUS - supremacy, DEADVITAL - validated, and LUCYCLAIR - crucially. Although there had been scant acknowledgement so far that the series coincided with the World Cup, I also went over those which had a football theme to them: AGLUMHOOT - goalmouth, GOALTRAIL - alligator, COLINREES - scoreline. If any of these came up my finger would depress that buzzer in a fraction of a second!

When round eleven began we were five minutes away from knowing the outcome. It was Paul's choice of letters, and it turned out to be a tricky selection. Paul's declaration that he had a six ('dreads') was followed by an anxious glance in my direction - but I could do no better. Once again we had used the same letters, although I had a different word ('adders'). Still there was deadlock at 86 points apiece. However, round twelve saw a breakthrough. I had struggled to what I thought was a safe six ('*cometh*'), whereas Paul declared a seven: 'telecom'. In fact my word was not acceptable; presumably '*cometh*' is considered so archaic as to have fallen into disuse. Susie suggested that it might be some consolation to me to learn that my word wasn't allowed. I smiled and shook my head: I would have preferred it to have been deemed valid - at least it would have scored some points if it had not been bettered.

A seven-point deficit was not disastrous. I had come from an identical position in the semi-final to win by eleven. The last letters round ensued, and Paul's choices provided another testing selection. For most of the thirty seconds I had difficulty getting beyond the six-letter word 'spaced': however, I noticed 'deacons' with a few seconds to spare, and was hopeful that I had at least done enough to tie the round. But Paul declared an eight! He had spotted a word worthy of the occasion: 'dyspnoea'. My heart sank. It was a word I knew, and I had noticed the possibility for creating words involving the syllable 'dys-' without recognising its full potential.

Carol looked dumbfounded as she put the word up on the board. It took Paul's score up to 101, and increased his advantage to 15. I knew now what I had to do if I was going to triumph. There were two rounds remaining: I had to win them both. It was a tall order, but it could be done. It fell to me to choose the numbers. I was determined to make light of my predicament, and demonstrate that, whatever happened, it would not put a damper on my sense of humour.

'Four from the top didn't really work last time, did it Carol?' I began. She agreed. 'So I'll try it again,' I concluded, to a ripple of amusement from the audience.

This time the four large numbers were supplemented by a 4 and a 3. I waited with bated breath for the target. If another easy one came out it was all over. When 880 showed up I knew I had a chance. I began looking for 4×220, but could only find 219 with which to make 876. I looked instead for 5×176: I could make either 5 or 176, but not both. The thirty seconds had expired. Des asked for my declaration first. I replied that I had 876, not written down, hoping that I would be able to recall how I had arrived at this figure if I got the chance to do so. Paul declared 882, which was closer, but it was clear that he was uncertain of his calculations.

Was I about to be let off the hook again? Paul got as far as $4 \times 75 = 300$, and took away 6, made by $50/25 \times 3$. This left 294: Paul just needed to multiply by 3 to make 882 and the contest was over. But all that was left was the 100. Carol recognised that he had used a number twice. So it was over to me to remember how to make 876!

I hesitated for a moment, before remembering that I had started with $3 \times 75 = 225$. Then I recalled that I had added the 100 to the 50 and divided the total by 25. There was relief in my voice as I identified that the resulting 6 could be subtracted from the 225, and that 219 multiplied by 4 would give 876.

It was perhaps the biggest test I had faced on Countdown, to go through a complex numbers game from memory, with defeat a certainty if I made a slip. I felt proud that I had managed to grab hold of the lifeline I had been thrown. It was, as Des said, a very special seven points. Paul's advantage had been reduced to eight and if I spotted the conundrum I could win by two!

The lights were dimmed, our fingers moved to our buzzers, and Des asked for the crucial Champion of Champions Conundrum to be revealed. I moved my head forward so that when the conundrum was turned over I would see it fractionally sooner. It was a tactic which had worked in the quarter-final, when Matt and I both saw 'soliloquy', but I was a split second ahead on the buzzer. I felt positive at this moment. I had believed from the start that I would have to spot a crucial conundrum in the final to clinch victory, and I was about to reap my reward for having prepared so thoroughly for it. One of 'my' conundrums was going to appear, and I would depress my buzzer so swiftly it would be impossible to beat me. 'DESINGOAL' was the most likely...

But it wasn't; it was 'PRONEPIPE'. It meant nothing to me. But then nor had 'GREATDRIP', so I knew not to despair. I set my mind went to work. I just had time to consider and

166

dismiss 'porcupine', before the sound I had not wanted to hear erupted. Even then I didn't give up. With the noise of Paul's buzzer ringing in my ears, I grabbed my pen. If Paul was wrong, as he had been in our previous final, I was going to give myself the maximum possible time in which to contemplate the letters in the form of a grid.

'Yes, Paul,' said Des.

'Pepperoni.'

I took one look at the letters and knew it was the right answer. There was no need to keep watching as the word was revealed on the monitor:

Pepperoni.

It could hardly have been a worse conundrum for me. Pepperoni is not a word that would spring to my mind. It's not something I would choose to eat, being one of the few things I don't really like. (I like it even less now!)

Paul raised his arms aloft in triumph. I said 'Well done' and shook his hand. Paul's performance was quite remarkable; he had scored the maximum available points in fourteen rounds out of fifteen, and was a worthy winner.

And so my dream was finally at an end. It had taken until the 15th and last round of the 15th and last game, for someone to have an unassailable lead over me. I had survived four crucial conundrums. A fifth proved one too many.

The moment one challenge was over a new one began: that of accepting defeat with dignity and in a sporting manner, and not allowing my disappointment to get the better of me. This proved surprisingly easy in the moments that followed. I had kept my emotions at bay in order to ensure that my performance was not impaired by nervousness or over-eagerness. In the closing minutes of the show I simply maintained this focus. It enabled me to remain cheerful and positive, to give my comments on the outcome, and express my gratitude to those involved calmly and in an upbeat manner.

After the show was over, I even managed to remember to give Des his conundrum. He took a look at it for a few seconds before giving up. I assured him that the answer was an everyday word which he would definitely know, and he tried again, but then asked me to provide the answer. I got the impression he prefers to leave that side of things to the contestants!

When I spoke to Paul, I reminded him about the conversation we had after the series 52 final, which had been remarkably appropriate to this moment. Paul said that he knew I would get to the final – which was more than I did!

Soon afterwards the 'lads' who had watched the final in the Green Room came through onto the stage. I was pleased that they all said 'Well done', rather than 'Hard luck', I was still feeling positive about having reached the final, and their comments suggested they felt I had done myself justice. I remember Conor saying he 'would have been thrashed', which is hard to believe!

Sue came over, and I apologised for not having obeyed her order. She had emerged from her 'Conundrum cocoon' for the final time, and was smiling bravely, concealing her disappointment admirably.

Official photos followed. As with the Series 52 final, there were various combinations of participants. I was pleased that

Conor and Paul Howe were asked back for one of the photos. I hope that gave them a little consolation for narrowly missing out on a place in the final.

My recollections of what followed are hazy. Lisa came over and congratulated me. She also told me in some detail about her experiences of reading 'A Nightmare in *Paradise'*, saying she had found it difficult to put down, which was gratifying to hear. Graham Nash, winner of the previous Champion of Champions series in 2003, who had been in the audience, came over and introduced himself, and we had a brief chat. I remember that as we were making our way out an elderly lady approached me in the corridor, asking me to place my autograph alongside those of Des and Carol. I felt quite heartened by that. Unlike the Series 52 final, there was no reception after the recordings, so we were soon on our way back to the hotel. Ideally we would have liked to spend a restful evening there. But we had our babysitters to consider and so had a short time in which to have farewell drinks in the hotel bar. The mood was jovial, although only a handful of the contestants were there at this point: Steve and Michelle, John and Cath, and John Mayhew. Lisa and Sharon also came to join us. But everyone else, including Paul and his dad, seemed to have vanished.

I remember struggling to find our way out of Leeds. A problematic journey back down the M1 delayed our arrival in London until after midnight. There was plenty to take my mind off my disappointment. But in the days that followed I relived the closing minutes of the final many times, thinking of what might have been. I know Sue did so too. And my 91-year-old grandmother said repeatedly to my parents: 'If only Mark had seen that last word . . . '

Not many people will ever come quite so close to a perfect outcome without actually achieving it. Sue told me she was convinced I was going to win. In reality I feel I had enjoyed quite a lot of luck in getting that close. I just needed one more stroke of luck, which failed to materialise.

And what if I had won? To what extent would I have felt able to celebrate? It would have been a cruel blow for Paul, if he had once again had one hand on the trophy only to have it snatched from his grasp. I thought I had a good idea of how he must have felt after the series 52 final, but now I have a much clearer picture. I think for me it is easier to deal with, partly because I am twice his age and less intense than he is, and partly because I had already experienced the elation of victory in a final.

As for the story, would the outcome have been so much more satisfying if I had won? Might it not have just made the ending to the second part a repeat performance of the end of the first? I have already shared the jubilation of victory. Now I have been able to convey the disappointment of an honourable failure. Although my original title for this book, 'Champion of Champions', went out the window, Sue soon suggested another one - and in my opinion it's more appropriate. We were talking about it during our journey back from Leeds, and agreed that something punchy was required. 'Something like crucial,' she said. 'Crucial!' I replied, 'that's it!' Not only is it highly relevant to a 'career' which had featured five 'crucial conundrums'; also it captures the essence of what competing at the highest level of Countdown is all about. One mistake, one lapse of concentration or loss of nerve, or even just one conundrum you hadn't anticipated: any of these can be crucial!

My thoughts quickly turned to the future. Within days I had emailed Damian to let him know of my intention to write about my experiences on the programme. He readily agreed to 'chisel away' at a foreword, and to feature the book on the programme to assist with promotion. Within two weeks of the final I had drafted the outline for the book proposal, and begun work on the text. I decided to start at the end, while recent events were fresh in my mind. I actually began with the moment of confirmation that the final crucial conundrum was indeed 'pepperoni', and then wrote the rest of the story of the Champion of Champions series, before returning to the beginning of the tale. I wrote the remainder chronologically.

It's impossible to overstate how exciting the whole experience of 'Planet Countdown' was. Even in the immediate aftermath of the final I was able to say with conviction that I had had a great time from start to finish, and that I would advise anyone who was thinking of applying not to hesitate. I still crave the thrill of being back in the studio, setting off in pursuit of the perfect score, savouring the excitement of taking on the best players and being able to compete with them. Other challenges remained: I learned through an email from Jono that there would be a Countdown event in Bristol later in the year, and I was involved in another hard-fought title decider with Chris Wills, who won on the second crucial conundrum after I had levelled the scores with the first! Also there was another COLIN early in 2007 – I came in third behind Chris Wills and Paul Howe.

These events counted towards a ranking system, ingeniously devised by Soo Reams; as yet the system is not officially recognised - although that might change, especially if Damian realises how high he is placed on the list! The best I have ever been is second behind Conor, but at some point I want to spend some time at number one in the list. Another challenge is to extend my longest sequence of winning runs when playing along at home (currently exactly 100 during series 55). And finally the possibility has crossed my mind that at some point Paul Gallen and I might be asked back to record a 'special' edition in which we played out a 'decider'. Personally I wouldn't actually seek out such an encounter: I feel that there is a sort of symmetry about our records which reflects the extent to which we were evenly matched. We each won 14 out of 15, and only ever lost to each other. I don't think another contest would prove anything either way. But if we *were* asked to do this . . . Well, I wouldn't duck the challenge, would I? Who knows, maybe this story hasn't quite reached its end yet, after all?

Advice for others wishing to improve their prowess at Countdown

Introduction

Now that you've read the account of my exploits on Countdown, you will know that it was the culmination of years of endeavour. I firmly believe that it was practice and a methodical approach, rather than some innate ability, which made it possible for me to realise my dream. Although there are no guarantees, I am confident that anyone who is able and willing to devote the considerable amount of time required to applying the techniques I am going to describe will have a good chance of an extended run of success on the show. However, I am well aware that many of those who have read my story will not be aspiring series champions, but may have set themselves other objectives. Before going any further, I recommend that you have a clear idea of what you would like to achieve. As a way of doing this, take a look at the following statements and see which is the most appropriate to you.

*I play along at home and would like improve, but have no wish to be a contestant on the show.

*I would just like the experience of appearing on the show, and am not too bothered how well I do.

*I would like to win at least one show, so that I can claim to have been a champion (and have the teapot to prove it).

*I would like to win a few games. If I made it to the quarter-finals or became an octavian, that would be great!

*I want to win as many games as possible, and will not be entirely satisfied with anything less than being an overall series champion.

*None of these; I'm just reading on out of interest!

It isn't hard to guess which of these statements I would have opted for had someone presented me with this selection before I embarked on my quest. Shortly before my first appearance on Countdown, I remember asking myself this: if I could settle right now for being overall runner-up in the series, would I do so? Would I forfeit my chance of becoming series champion in order to ensure that I didn't fall by the wayside early on? The answer would definitely have been 'no'. That's not to say that if I had finished runner-up, I wouldn't have gone home with considerable satisfaction at the achievement, just as was the case after the Champion of Champions series. But I wouldn't have compromised my objective from the outset.

If your aspirations are modest, implementing the straightforward parts of the advice which follows should go a long way towards enabling you to achieve them. On the other hand, if you want to compete with the best, you will need to commit as much time as possible to practice and preparation. I wouldn't be able to begin to quantify the number of hours I spent improving my prowess at the game, especially as there were countless occasions when I snatched the opportunity to spend the odd few minutes - or even the odd few seconds - doing something which contributed to this end. I had the good fortune to have a lifestyle that enabled me to do this, to an extent that would have been impossible for many people. My work for the Royal Mail, whilst requiring self-discipline and good organisational skills, was not so absorbing of my time and energy as to leave me feeling drained at the end of the day. Being out on the road most of the time requires a sensible number of rest breaks, and I was able to use these to practise, utilising the cards from the Countdown box set, or the pocket-sized squares about which I will give more detail below.

I was lucky, too, that my girlfriend Sue supported me in what I wanted to achieve. Without her understanding and patience it would have been much more difficult, perhaps even impossible.

In a nutshell, if you have a stressful job, or highly demanding domestic commitments, or if there is something else in your life that is likely to hamper your progress, I would recommend that you either modify your expectations, or put your Countdown ambitions on hold until such time as the path to success is clearer.

Section 1

Monitoring your progress

Watching the show

At the risk of stating the obvious, there is no substitute for watching the show regularly - every day if possible. I recommend videoing the show, even if you are able to watch it live. You can then pause it if there are any distractions such as a knock at the door, or if you come across a word of which you are uncertain and wish to check before carrying on. If you have serious aspirations, I recommend that you use the correct dictionary, at the time of writing the second edition of the *Oxford Dictionary of English* (*ODE*), currently priced at £35.

<u>Playing along</u>

It's important not only to play along, but also to see how your score compares with those of the contestants. How you get on will offer you a good guide to how likely you are to pass an audition. If you never beat the contestants you need to be realistic and accept that you will need to improve in order to stand a chance. If you beat some people, but not others, you have a good chance of passing an audition, and if that is your goal then it's probably time to have a go. If, however, you want to challenge the top contenders, then you will need regularly to outscore most of the contestants. Inevitably those who are themselves in with a chance of becoming series champions (usually the top three or four seeds of each series) will be of a comparable standard. But you shouldn't lose heavily to anyone - if you do so, take it as a warning sign that you still have some way to go!

<u>Keeping score</u>

When you are playing along at home, you have two opponents instead of one. The simplest way of scoring is to have three columns in which you keep cumulative totals for each of the three players. As on the show, only the best answer, or joint best, scores points. You will therefore often end up with a lower score than you would have achieved if you had been playing only one of the contestants. If you want to be thorough, you can always go back over the game and see what you would have scored if you had been playing just one contestant.

At the end of each round, I recommend that you always make your decision about what to declare before *either* of the contestants on the show reveals their answer. It's simpler that way, because you don't have to decide at what point in the process your turn to declare falls. Also your score would only ever have been *better* if you were actually playing on the show, because when you declare second you may have the opportunity to use tactics as described below.

The 'Max Factor'

In a separate column of your scorecard, keep a running total of the maximum points available. Usually if neither of the contestants spot the best answer, Susie or Carol will enlighten them, but this is not always so; it is quite feasible to come up with a word or a solution that nobody on the show has noticed. If you have the time, the enthusiasm, and the technology, I would recommend regular visits to www.thecountdowncorral.com (a Soo Reams website). Features include an ever-growing database, comprising reviews of episodes of Countdown. On it you will find details of 'Dictionary Corner beaters' – words which nobody spotted at the time.

Beside the entry in the maximum column put a Y for yes or an N for no, according to whether or not you managed to get the best possible score in that round. At the end of the programme count up the number of Ys, and you will see how many times out of fifteen you obtained the maximum. Expressed as a fraction, I call this the 'max' factor. Keep a record of the 'max' factors you have scored over a period of time. This is the most reliable guide as to how much you are improving - unlike your total score, it will not be influenced by the calibre of your opponents.

Below is an example of a simple scorecard, which I have filled in with the results of a recent episode I watched. You can, of course, set a template of this scorecard on a computer and print off a supply of them. Alternatively, you can be like me and scribble a new one each day on the back of an envelope! As recommended above, all scores are recorded cumulatively.

Maximum achieved Y/N?	Maximum Score Available	Contestant A	Contestant B	Self
Y	7	0	0	7
N	25	18	0	7
Y	32	25	7	14
Y	50	25	7	32
Y	60	35	17	42
Y	67	42	17	49
Y	75	50	17	57
N	83	56	23	63
N	90	56	23	69
Y	100	66	23	79
N	108	66	31	79
N	114	72	31	79
Y	122	72	31	87
Y	132	82	41	97
N	142	82	51	97
Y = 9, N = 6				

<u>Considering the 'worst case scenario'.</u>

It is fairly easy to look back and see how many points you would have scored if you had the exceptional misfortune to come up against an outstanding contestant who spotted everything. All you need do is add up the points you scored in the rounds where you placed a Y in the 'Maximum achieved?' column, and then see how it compares with the total you have already computed for the maximum. Don't include the conundrum in your score even if you got it: assume that the expert you came up against beat you to it! Try not to let the results of this exercise get you down. Most of the contestants who appear on the show would obtain quite low scores on this basis.

<u>Charting your progress</u>

One way of monitoring the extent to which you are improving is to compile a graph showing your max factors and/or your total scores over time. The 'y' axis should be used for the scores, and the 'x' axis for time. Plot your scores on the graph and join up the dots in a line. If the general trend of the line (or the 'line of best fit', if you are a statistician) points upwards to the right, you are still improving. If it levels out you have reached your potential. Personally I doubt whether anyone who carries on trying ever stops improving altogether, but there comes a time when the improvement will be too slight to show up on a graph.

<u>Other simple records</u>

It is also useful to keep a record of words you missed, especially if they were unfamiliar to you. This helps reinforce them in your memory, and makes it less likely that you will miss them again next time they come up. Having a look back at a record of this kind would be an excellent final preparation for an audition, or an appearance on the programme.

Keep a note of your longest winning sequence. I suggest classifying a 'win' as an occasion when you would have beaten both the contestants on the programme. But you could argue that if you would have beaten the champion in the previous day's game, you should only have to hold off the challenger, as that is how it would work if you were actually a contestant. Once your winning sequence ends, start again and try to extend your record.

Section 2

<u>Tips for letters games.</u>

<u>Anticipation</u>

It is second nature to see what words you can spot from the letters as they appear. I've never come across anyone who doesn't do that! But try to go beyond that, to anticipate words which are likely to come up given the selection so far, especially if all that is required is one more vowel or one of the more regular consonants.

<u>Avoid limiting your options</u>

When you're playing along at home, you are stuck with whatever the contestants choose. If you are a regular viewer, you may have had the experience of seeing an eight letter word from the first eight letters, and realised that all that was needed was an 's' for a nine-letter word. You might have sat there urging the wavering player to choose a consonant, only to have your hopes dashed when they finally opted for a vowel! When playing the board game, playing on-line, or when you're actually on the show, you have the opportunity to influence the play. But bear in mind the rule which states that your selection must contain at least four consonants and at least three vowels. The consequence is that you will definitely end up with the next four letters in the consonant pile, and the next three letters in the vowel pile. So seven of the nine letters are effectively predetermined, and you actually only choose the last two! What's more, you are left with only three possible combinations of letters: two more consonants, two more vowels, or one more of each. The only other influence you have is that you determine the order in which the letters appear.

It therefore makes sense, when choosing your letters, to ensure that the first seven choices comprise four consonants and three vowels. Otherwise you are restricting your choices still further. If, for example, you choose five consonants before you select any vowels, then three of your remaining four choices must be vowels, and only one choice is down to you. Put another way, you will have eliminated the possibility of a five-vowel selection before you've even set eyes on the first of the vowels.

One way of ensuring that your first seven choices comprise four consonants and three vowels is to stick to a pattern. It doesn't have to be an obvious pattern, such as starting with a consonant and alternating consonants and vowels: it could be two consonants, three vowels, then two more consonants. However, if you feel confident that you won't lose track of how many of each you have selected, I recommend that you

181

make your choices spontaneously. As you might have noticed if you saw the shows in which I was involved, I like to be unpredictable in my choices! I don't think my opponents ever knew quite what I was likely to opt for (especially when it came to the numbers games). I think that the element of surprise sometimes gave me a slight advantage.

6 consonant selections

These yield fewer nine-letter words than selections containing five consonants and four vowels, although there are some useful 'regulars' among them, some of which don't occur often in real life: 'transomed', 'dipterans', 'dicentras', 'therapsid' and 'spermatid' are among them. Selections involving six consonants are a good choice if you have an in-depth knowledge of allowable agent nouns or are familiar with the many rarely used verbs to be found in the *ODE*. Look out for '-ed' and '-er' or 're-'. Also remember that a 'y' can be the middle letter of a syllable, effectively taking the place of an 'i' in words such as 'dyslexia', 'sympodium', 'syndicate' and 'hendiadys'. Paul Gallen's 'dyspnoea' en route to winning our Champion of Champions final is another example.

The 'classic selection' – five consonants, four vowels.

The guidance notes which Countdown issues to contestants prior to their appearance recommend this selection, on the basis that it tends to yield longer words. In practice the majority of selections turn out to be five consonants and four vowels, even if the contestants don't always set out to achieve this! The overwhelming majority of nines are formed from this selection, including arguably the most common nine on the programme, 'delations'. Other regulars

182

include: 'creations'/ 'narcotise'/ 'reactions'/ 'actioners', 'ordinates'/ 'notarised'/ 'derations', 'patronise'/ 'isopteran' and 'steroidal'/ 'idolaters'.

Appendix 1 lists 110 'nines you must not miss' (I couldn't quite get it down to 100), and for those who want to be really competitive appendix 2 lists all the nine-letter words I could find comprising five different consonants and four different vowels. There are also plenty of regular nines comprising five consonants and four vowels where the only duplication involves one of the vowels: 'datelines'/'dentalise' is a good example. Look closely at these nine letters and you'll see that the only difference between this combination and 'delations' is the second 'e' in place of the 'o'. If on the other hand it were the 'i' that were duplicated this would yield 'disentail'. If you watch the programme regularly you will become accustomed to seeing these words unfolding before your eyes as the selection progresses. During the Champion of Champions series those of us who watched in the Green Room amused ourselves by guessing which of the 'regulars' might result after the first few letters had been chosen. I would say that anyone who wants to have a chance of competing with the best *must* know all the 'nines you must not miss'.

Five - vowel selections

In practice the vast majority of contestants opt for either three or four vowels. However, if you have a particularly strong vocabulary a five-vowel selection can be advantageous, as it opens up the possibility of finding words which don't usually feature on the programme, and which are therefore less likely to be known to your opponent. It was the choice of a fifth vowel which enabled me to spot 'ipomoea' and so clinch victory in the first round of the Champion of Champions series. Another situation in which you may want to choose a fifth vowel is when your consonant selection has produced a 'q', although the letter distribution is such that the chances of getting a 'u' among a 5-vowel selection aren't that great. On the other hand, you might be lucky enough to generate nine-letter words; examples of these might be 'aliquotes' or 'aliquoted', or 'ortanique'/'inquorate'.

The choice of a fifth vowel can also be a tactical move. For example, imagine a game in which you have a 28-point lead with three rounds to play, and it's your choice of letters. The only way back for your opponent is to win that round with at least an eight-letter word. They would still need to win the last numbers game, and then guess the conundrum to tie the scores, and so force a second conundrum. You are in a very strong, but not unassailable position. Say your initial seven selections were to produce the following: C V O I K A N. Even at a glance you can see that choosing two more vowels would make it highly unlikely that the selection will yield an eight-letter word, which leaves you in an unbeatable position even if you don't win that particular round. However, if you were to choose a more conventional selection (say another vowel and one more consonant), you could run into trouble. For example, an 'e' and an 'r' would offer 'veronica', which is fine provided you spot it, but if you don't and your opponent *does* you may let them off the hook.

<u>Writing down the letters</u>

How many times have you seen a contestant declare a correctly spelt word, only to have it disallowed because they have either used a letter which wasn't there, or used a letter more than once? Even top players can do this: in my Champion of Champions series semi-final I was gifted a seven-point lead right at the start when Paul Howe declared 'carnage' from a selection containing a single 'a'. Many such errors can be put down to nerves, an aspect of the challenge to which I will return later. But there are other reasons: mishearing letters, misreading letters on the screen (or on the board in the case of contestants on the show), carelessness, seeing 'phantom letters' due to wishful thinking, or not having time to check a word that you think you've spotted at the last gasp.

It is obviously important to ensure that any hearing or visual difficulties of which you are aware have been properly rectified prior to making an appearance on the show. As Carol makes allowances for the hard of hearing when pronouncing letters - you may have noticed that she is particularly careful to distinguish between 'm' and 'n' - you should have no reason to mishear letters. This is equally true when you're playing along at home, provided of course that the television is set at an appropriate volume! Anyone with properly adjusted vision should have no difficulty reading the letters on the screen.

On the show itself contestants have a monitor inset in the desk. I would recommend using it to watch Carol put the letters on the board, rather than looking across the room at the real thing - especially if you're short-sighted.

The most effective way of ensuring that you end up with the right set of letters is to allow what you see to reinforce what you hear, rather than relying solely on either your eyes or your ears. That way, you are unlikely to make any mistakes.

Another error contestants sometimes make is to write down a letter poorly and subsequently misread it. Practise writing precisely using capital letters. Be especially careful to distinguish 'U's from 'V's, and 'O's from 'Q's.

As for careless errors, the only way to eliminate these is to develop your powers of concentration through practice. Later in this section I will recommend the approach of alternating between looking at the letters as you've written them down, and looking back at the screen. If you do this you will find that you tend to spot any inconsistencies. Also your familiarity with the letters that *are* actually there will be enhanced to the extent that it will preclude the possibility of using any bogus letters.

The most difficult problem to overcome is that of the word you've spotted with one second to go before the music stops. You haven't had time to check it, let alone write it down. Although the rules of Countdown state that you should stop working when the thirty seconds are up, in practice a moment's hesitation while you satisfy yourself that your word really is there will not be frowned upon. It is important to think quickly; again, this comes with practice. Make sure you know what your back-up word is, and how long it is, so that if you realise you have made a mistake you will still have a chance to score.

The grid system

When writing down the letters, it is important to be systematic. There is no point at all in writing down the letters in a row, keeping them in the same order in which they came out. I use the 'grid system'. This involves setting the letters out in three columns of three. I recommend keeping vowels mainly in the middle column. Some consonants tend to occur at the beginning of words: 'b', 'f' and 'p' are the most notable. Keep these in the left hand column. Other consonants tend to occur at the end of words: 't', 'y' and 's' are examples. Keep these in the right hand column. The remaining letters can be used to fill the gaps in the grids. By doing this you are more likely to find that complete syllables fall into place. Consider this example:

R C A I L T E S P

If you rearrange the letters as prescribed above, it's a lot easier to spot that this selection yields a nine-letter word. Have a look at the grid:

P A R

C I T

L E S

See the footnote at the end of this section if you are still unsure of the 'nine'.

Here's another example:

L I F E S I N A S

The choice of a fourth vowel means that one of them will have to be put in either the left or right columns, as the middle column is full.

Here is one possible grid formation:

F I L
A I S
N E S

Again a nine-letter word is possible, as given in the footnote at the end of this section.

This technique can be used to solve conundrums, although I certainly wouldn't recommend using it as a matter of course. Give yourself at least a few seconds to see it first. If you do decide to use a grid, you will have to work quickly, and not be too particular about what letter goes where. You will recall how I described what happened in my series 52 final when my opponent Paul Gallen buzzed after one second, only to realise that he was mistaken. With the rest of the time to myself, I contemplated 'GREATDRIP' for no more than another couple of seconds before grabbing a pen, and hastily scribbling down the letters in the form of a grid. Although I didn't keep the piece of paper I used, I know that the result would have looked much like this:

P A R

G I T

R E D

By the time I had finished scribbling I had a little over fifteen seconds left in which to consider the result, which proved just enough to see the word 'partridge'!

Since the series 52 final I have refined the grid system, so that the following letters are placed, as far as possible, in 'regular' places.

P: top left

D: bottom left

E: bottom middle

I: central to the grid

T: middle right

S: bottom right

Other letters and duplicates of the above are placed in the remaining slots.

So a selection containing one of each of the above and three (unspecified) other letters would give rise to a grid like this:

P ? ?

? I T

D E S

This formation keeps the letter 'p', the most common of the 'letters normally found at the start of the word' in the best place for spotting words beginning with 'p'. The letter 's', which of course is commonly added to the end of nouns and verbs, is placed in the position which the English reader would naturally consider the 'last'. The formation also makes it relatively easy to spot words ending in '-iest' or '-ise(d)', as well as words beginning 'de-' or ending '-ed'.

Although the grid system is a useful tool, it is not foolproof. It is important not to overlook the possibility that the grid may be structured in such a way that long words may be hidden within it. Here's an example of a nine-letter word that doesn't show up well:

S G U R I N A E T

Using the grid system, you might come up with this arrangement:

G U R

A I T

N E S

An additional problem with this example is that there are a lot of promising looking part-words: '-iest', '-age(s)', '-ate(s)', '-iate(s)', '-ant(s)', 'in-' and 're-'. In fact the answer involves none of these. Again, see the footnote if you have given up on it!

<u>Look back at the screen</u>

I have already recommended that you alternate between looking at the grid and looking at the row of letters on the screen. A second reason for doing this is that if you concentrate exclusively on the grid it is easy to miss words or part-words which might be more or less spelt out in the original line-up. This occurred to me when watching the transmission of one of my series 52 games. My opponent Keith Jones won a round with the seven-letter word 'traffic' (beating my six, 'fiacre'). Sue remembered hearing someone near her in the audience expressing their disbelief that I hadn't seen 'traffic'. When I looked at the order in which the letters had emerged, I could see what they meant. From that moment on I resolved to foster the habit of spending at least a small part of each thirty seconds contemplating the nine letters as they are manifested on the screen.

Take another look at the final example of the grid system given in the section immediately above. Now compare it with the row of letters from which it was compiled. You will probably agree that it is much easier to spot the nine-letter word by looking at the original line-up.

<u>Spotting '-ing' words</u>

It is relatively easy to spot words containing the '-ing' suffix. Usually such words are the present participle form of a verb (frequently occurring as an adjective; e.g. 'the barking dog'), though they can sometimes be nouns ('swimming is good for you'). If the letters 'i', 'n' and 'g' appear in the selection, see if you can use the remaining six letters to form a verb, thereby making a nine. If you can't see a six-letter verb, look instead for a five-letter or four-letter verb, not forgetting that verbs often double the consonant before '-ing' ('swimming' again), as I explain in more detail below. Most people who have reached the standard required to appear as contestants will have mastered this technique, so you will be lucky if such a word proves to be a winner.

<u>Verbs ending in '-e'</u>

Remember that many seven-letter verbs ending in 'e' drop the last letter when the suffix is added. Examples include 'lecture', 'receive', and 'provide'. This also applies to shorter verbs such as 'escape', 'refute', and 'induce'. If you find that you often miss such words, here is a technique you might want to try:

Leaving aside the 'i', 'n' and 'g', arrange the other six letters in a circle set apart from the grid. Then put an 'e' beside or beneath them, and use this template to look for verbs. It will need to be done rapidly, and you need to be sure not to include the extra 'e' in the word you produce.

Here's an example:

I R N V E A L T G

or in grid form:

G   A   R

V   I   T

L   E   N

Using the method described above:

   R   L

V   T

   E   A

     E

Notice that I have made the additional 'e' larger than the other letters. This acts as a reminder not to use it in your solution. In this example, you must avoid the mistake of incorporating it into the word 'revealing'!

With luck, the reduced grid will have enabled you to spot the six-letter verb, 'relate'. As this loses the second 'e' when '-ing' is added, you therefore have five letters to combine with '-ing', to make the eight-letter word 'relating'. If you look back at the original selection you can check your findings. Eight of the nine letters have been used once each: only the 'v' remains unused.

Verbs ending in a single consonant

Another thing to remember when searching for '-ing' words is that if the infinitive of the verb ends in a single consonant its present continuous form will *usually* double that consonant. Examples include 'putting' and 'tipping'. You are more likely to spot these from the normal nine-letter grid, or the original line of letters, because when you are using the modified grid you will be concentrating on finding verbs which *lose* their final letter. So try to make use of everything you have available to you. Sometimes if you cast your eye back you will see something at a glance which you missed the first time.

Verbs ending '-s'

Verbs ending in 's' can sometimes add a second 's' before the '-ing', in some cases as an alternative to a single 's': for example, 'focusing' and 'focussing' are both acceptable. You can also have 'busing' and 'bussing', along with 'embusing' and 'embussing', as it is all right to use one 's' or two with participles of the infinitive 'embus' (to get on a bus); however, 'debussing' *must* take the second 's', as the verb is conjugated strictly as follows: 'debu<u>s</u>, debu<u>s</u>es, debu<u>ss</u>ing, debu<u>ss</u>ed'. (Don't blame me – I didn't compile the *ODE*!)

Adding an 's' on the end of '-ing' words

Contestants often attempt to pluralise '-ing' words. Usually such a declaration is accompanied by the comment that the word is 'risky', a remark which is only too well founded. It is only acceptable to pluralise words which are specifically listed as nouns. Those in the dictionary tend to be words which are a regular part of everyday life, such as 'fittings', 'fixings' and 'wordings'. In short, if you come up with an 's' word which sounds plausible, but you can't recall hearing it used, it's best left alone. Appendix 5 shows '–ing' words which can be pluralised.

Bear in mind when perusing selections (or conundrums) that contain the letters 'i', 'n' and 'g' that there are plenty of words that use these letters as separate entities (not as '-ing' words). Here are just a few examples: 'longitude', 'magnitude', 'genocidal', 'ignoblest', 'navigated' and 'angelfish'. For a fuller list, see appendix 4.

General points regarding letters games

Don't give the game away

You might be lucky enough to see a nine right at the start of the thirty seconds. If you're playing along at home, you can afford to relax, provided you are certain you are right. But when competing on the show itself, it's not a good idea to sit back and look pleased with yourself! Even if your opponent is deep in thought, they may sense that you aren't. This will offer a fair indication that you have seen a nine, which in turn may encourage them to spot it too.

Be methodical

As the selection evolves, jot down the longest word you can see, even if it's only a four or a five. If something longer occurs to you, write that down. Concentration and the ability to write quickly but accurately are essential. Practice is the key. Bear in mind that sometimes all you will need to do is add an 's' or '-ed' to your existing word.

Once all nine letters are in place, take a quick look to see if there is a nine staring you in the face. If not, but you can see an eight, write that down, and then spend the rest of the time searching for a nine. Otherwise go back to the longest word you have already spotted and try to better it. Bear in mind that if you can't find a word that is just one letter longer than the word you already have, you might have more luck searching for something longer still. For example, if you have a five, and can't find a six, try looking instead for a seven.

Unless you have a nine, (or an eight in a selection containing a 'q' but no 'u') carry on looking right to the end of the thirty seconds. You may think you have already seen the longest word available from the selection, but you could be wrong!

Avoid ending up in a situation where you have nothing at all to declare. Contestants sometimes realise at the last moment that they have made a mistake, and have no back-up word. If you have adopted the methodical approach recommended above, this shouldn't happen to you. However poor a selection is, you should be able to see *something* at a glance. Don't be afraid to declare a very short word. Your opponent might be stumped, too, or may offer a word which is disallowed. Rounds have been won with three-letter words. Declare three, two or even one if necessary! It may give you the points that ultimately make the difference between winning and losing.

'Risky' words

Introduction

There are various reasons why words might be considered risky. You might be certain that a word exists, but unsure as to whether you have spelt it correctly, whether it is capitalised, or whether its use in the plural is legitimate (see below regarding mass nouns). You may be unsure whether the word you have seen is hyphenated, or whether it should in fact be two separate words. Alternatively you may have come up with a word which sounds plausible, but you have no idea whether it is listed in the dictionary. In some instances you may arrive at such a word without having a clue as to its possible meaning!

Strategies for minimising reliance on risky words

Thorough preparation

Ensuring that you have a high degree of familiarity with the *ODE* (see below) is the best way to avoid being left in a quandary, because you will more readily recognise the really speculative words for what they are and dismiss them accordingly. When a contestant offers something to which Susie replies, 'I don't think so', you can be virtually certain it won't be in the dictionary, even though she will take the precaution of checking. If you are prepared to go to the lengths required to obtain such in-depth knowledge, you will also have the benefit of feeling confident that words of which you have never heard are most unlikely to be listed. Still further contingencies will arrive that will test your memory and judgement. For example, you may have to determine whether you can add a comparative and superlative ending ('-er'/'-ier', and '-est'/'-iest') to a two-syllable adjective such as 'stupid' (yes, you can) or 'pursy' (no, you can't). Or you may have to decide whether the plural of 'halo' is 'halos' or 'haloes' (it can be either). However good your memory, it's almost impossible to eliminate risk altogether.

<u>Assessing risky words</u>

If you see a word of which you are unsure early on in the thirty seconds, avoid spending too long deliberating on whether to risk it. Scribble it down, so that you don't forget it; then keep looking to see what else you can come up with - even if it's only a word of the same length, but less risky. If you end up having to revert to the doubtful word, you may find that you have mysteriously become clearer in your mind about whether or not it's likely to be accepted. I'm not an expert on the subconscious, but I would guess it's a bit like the recommended technique for passing exams: read the whole paper before attempting any of the questions, so that when you do start writing, your subconscious can set to work on the ones you have yet to answer!

If your risky word is longer than anything else you've spotted, try to make sure your longest 'safe' word is written down too, so that if you decide against the risky word, you still have something demonstrable to fall back on.

The most difficult situation to deal with is when you see a word you have doubts about right at the end of the thirty seconds. All you can do is follow your 'gut reaction' to the word. The chances are you will be right.

The tactical 'risk'

Sometimes contestants who are trailing declare risky words in an attempt to reduce the deficit. Prudent judgement is required as to when it is appropriate to use this tactic. For example, if your opponent spots a nine in the very first round, and you miss it, don't throw caution to the wind. Your opponent may not be so hot when it comes to the numbers games: it only takes a ten-point win to reduce the advantage to eight points and so put you right back within striking distance. You might also find that the first round outcome was not indicative of the game as a whole. And there is always the possibility that you may later win a letters game with a nine of your own, and so cancel out the effect of the first round. My series 52 game against Ronnie Boyd, described earlier, provides an example of how a game can turn right around after a nightmare start!

Very often, declaring a risky word when you are behind only has the effect of increasing the deficit. My series 52 match against Keith Jones offers an example of a situation where 'riskiness' played an important part, notably in the first letters game of the final part of the show. Keith declared first, stating that he had a 'risky six'. My choice lay between a risky five, 'gamma', and a safe four, 'game'. Keith had just won the second numbers game to reduce my lead to nineteen. I was conscious that, as things stood, if Keith could repeat this feat in the last numbers game, it would lead to a crucial conundrum - something I had so far managed to avoid! Although I felt fairly confident that the word 'gamma' was in the dictionary, I decided to stick with the safer word. My reasoning was as follows: if Keith's six turned out to be valid, it would be irrelevant whether I declared five or four. If, however, he were mistaken, I would be certain of a 23-

point lead with four rounds to play - a very healthy position to be in. My lead would have been only marginally more comfortable if I had declared my risky word and it turned out to be correct.

Keith's word (*'gammel'*) was in fact a speculative attempt. So the outcome was that I secured another four points with my safe word. In fact 'gamma' *is* allowable, so I could have scored five points. But I would have kicked myself if I had risked it, and discovered that it wasn't listed. Neither of us would have increased our totals, and I would have been left with the relatively fragile 19-point lead.

<u>Summary</u>

I recommend that you avoid risking words you are uncertain of in the hope that they *might* be in the dictionary, unless you have absolutely no choice. You should always think hard before taking a chance on words which, for whatever reason, you are unsure of.

<u>Footnote</u>

R C A I L T E S P = Particles

L I F E S I N A S = Finalises

S G U R I N A E T = Signature

Section 3

Expanding your vocabulary

Introduction

In the advice given earlier in this section I concentrated on techniques for spotting words with which you are familiar. It stands to reason that you will only be able to see words you know. Unless you have a truly remarkable vocabulary, it makes sense to actively seek out new words. Reading avidly is helpful, but I am firmly of the opinion that the only way to compete with the best is to familiarise yourself with the 'answer book': the second edition of the *ODE*, to which I have frequently referred.

Using the dictionary for preparation

At 2,054 pages in length, the very sight of the *ODE* may be enough to put you off! It certainly can't be slipped into your briefcase or handbag. Even if you are dedicated enough to take it with you on holiday, you might struggle to find room for it in your suitcase! And then there's the fact that the *ODE* lists and defines over 100,000 words! If, despite all this, you are determined to ingest the book and make it part of your metabolism, you may well have what it takes to realise your aspirations! After all, there is some good news . . .

If you are studying the *ODE* solely for the purpose of enhancing your prowess at Countdown, you can afford to overlook the following: words comprising ten or more letters; words containing hyphens (including for instance the vast majority of the hundreds of words beginning with the prefix 'self-'); words which are capitalised; and words with which you are already familiar. Furthermore, the fact that you are enthusiastic enough about Countdown to read *this* book suggests you have more than a passing interest in the English language; it is, therefore, likely that you will find your efforts rewarding, interesting and even pleasurable. Finally, by breaking the task down into manageable chunks, you can make it seem a great deal less onerous.

Setting yourself a schedule

Imagine you have passed your audition and have been notified of a recording date which is four months away. If you look through twenty pages per day in the meantime you can get right through the dictionary with a couple of weeks to spare. If you decide you can afford an hour per day for your preparation, you will have an average of three minutes per page. As each page of the dictionary is divided into three columns, you can devote an average of one minute to each column.

Of course, there may be the occasional day when circumstances prevent you from spending the allotted time on your endeavours. If you know you have the resolve required to catch up, then it won't matter; otherwise it is a good idea to allow for this when drawing up your schedule.

Methods for learning words

If you are lucky enough to possess the ability to remember everything you read at the first attempt then you will have a huge advantage over the rest of us. You will be able to achieve the same results as other people with far less input. On the other hand, perhaps you are more like me. I sometimes remember new words straight away, and retain them indefinitely, particularly if they are interesting. But there are others that I know I must have seen any number of times, but they still appear as strangers.

An example of a word which impressed me immediately and which has stayed in my mind is the bizarre adverb 'bovinely'. (When was the last time you saw someone perform an act in a bovine manner?) It is precisely this word's apparent absurdity which enabled it to shoulder its way into my memory. Another feature that makes a word more likely to stick is when it has a particularly interesting or enlightening definition. 'Dulosis' was a word which I learnt easily: I had no idea that there was such a thing as slavery among ants!

A further advantage of understanding the meaning or etymology of a word is that you will know to what extent you can vary the form in which the word appears in the dictionary. For example, if you know that a word is a verb you will be aware that (given the appropriate letters) you will be able to enhance it by adding verbal endings. Also, if it is a mass noun you will know that it is unlikely that you will be able to pluralise it, unless it is a 'dish' which can be segregated into portions.

It therefore makes sense, when studying the dictionary for the purpose of learning words for Countdown, for you to examine the definitions, instead of just adding a meaningless word to your vocabulary. I need hardly add that such a practice will also be of much greater educational benefit.

I find that the words which are most difficult to absorb are those which mean least to me. If a word has a definition which I don't understand, as is often the case with scientific terms, I am forced to settle for remembering how to spell it, and (if it is a noun) to know whether it is possible to add an 's' on the end. With scientific words certain endings give you clues towards this. Words ending in '-ite' or '-ase' are likely to be minerals or enzymes, which are mass nouns and therefore not to be pluralised. On the other hand, words ending with '-ate' or '-ide' are compounds, which can be pluralised. Most scientific words ending in '-ium' or '-ine' are chemical elements (such as 'barium', helium', 'bromine' and 'fluorine'), which don't usually allow for plurals: an exception is 'chlorine'.

A useful technique for memorising words is to pair them off on the basis of some kind of association, such as similar or opposite meanings. For instance, at some point during my preparation it occurred to me to link the words 'philobat' and 'ocnophil', on the basis of their contrasting meanings: the former is a risk-taker, the latter has an aversion to danger. As another example, I paired two noteworthy nines, 'tritanope' and 'protanope', both of which refer to someone who suffers from colour blindness. Establishing such associations is helpful because it adds an element of interest to the subject matter and thereby reinforces it in your memory.

If you are really committed to being thorough, as you work through the dictionary you can compile lists of useful words. Such lists might comprise groups of words according to a common prefix, suffix or origin.

The cosmopolitan nature of modern English language and culture means that words from all over the world have been imported into the dictionary. It is often easy to see why. If you walk through the average high street you will see restaurants representing a kaleidoscope of cultures: French,

Italian, Spanish, Mexican, Greek, Indian, Chinese, Malaysian, Tai, Japanese, Turkish, Russian, Lebanese, Jamaican, Afro-Caribbean . . . Words such as 'croissant', 'tandoori', 'ravioli' and 'kebab' are commonplace, but even less well known ones have found a home in Countdown's answer book. 'Rigatoni' and 'bresaola' are examples that appeared on the show during 2006, 'bresaola' contributing eight points to Conor's narrow win over John Brackstone in the Champion of Champions quarter-final.

It's not only food that has helped to feed the insatiable maw of the English language: music, technology and world events have all contributed. Again, it's not only those words which have become familiar in recent years, such as 'glasnost', 'tsunami', or 'satnav' that are listed. Numerous words that most of us will never have heard of are there, too: 'mridangam' (an African drum), 'thekedar' (an Indian contractor) and 'dazibao' (a Chinese propaganda poster) are examples.

Sometimes it's quite puzzling why a word has merited inclusion at all. For example, what are 'gemütlich' (German for cheerful) and 'cojones' (Spanish for bull's testicles – another word to have featured on Countdown in 2006) doing in an English dictionary?

During the course of my endeavours I compiled lists of dozens of words which are acceptable on Countdown. Examples of these can be found in the appendices to this book. Lists according to prefix are less useful, because they largely replicate words that can be found on the relevant page or pages of the dictionary; however, sometimes words with a common prefix are separated in the dictionary by others which coincidentally start with the same letters. Lists according to suffix can be very enlightening. Consider the list of words ending '-line' or '-lines' (appendix 10). I would never have expected to find as many as 47 words on this list. The letter distribution used on Countdown is such that the words on this list are particularly likely to occur. The same can be said of words ending in '-ness', '-ist(s)' and '-head'. Two of the nine-letter words I spotted during my appearances on the programme ('loftiness' and 'printhead') appeared on lists I had made, although their familiarity was reinforced by the 'squares' I used to practise with, as described further below.

Looking through the lists in the appendices would certainly be useful preparation for an audition or appearance on Countdown; however, if you have serious aspirations of competing with the best, I would recommend that you set about compiling your own lists from scratch.

One more comment I would make about lists is that it is both more enjoyable and more productive if you use your imagination. Appendix 12 contains my list of words that sound like someone's name, but aren't. Examples such as 'amyloid', 'allanite', 'crispate' and 'soubrette' - words that were otherwise completely unknown to me - stuck in my mind as a result of compiling this list. Similarly, Appendix 11 comprises a list of surnames that feature in the dictionary because they also have meaning. Such lists turned out to be surprisingly long, and were among the most interesting to assemble.

Another way of gleaning useful words from the dictionary is to work through it with different coloured highlighter pens, marking words which fall into a category on which you have identified a need to focus. Take care to do this neatly, making small but clear marks sufficiently close to the word concerned for the association to be obvious when you look back at your endeavours at a later date. Avoid obscuring the word you are highlighting, and above all do not use black ink. The print in the dictionary is quite small, and it is important not to make any marks on the text which might make it harder to read.

One carelessly placed mark might easily have cost me victory in the series 52 final. You may recall how I ventured a nine, ('*internets*') in the latter stages of the game in an attempt to turn a 5-point deficit into a 13-point advantage. Although my doubt concerned the plural, the word was actually disallowed because the entry in the dictionary is capitalised. Afterwards I looked to see why I hadn't noticed the initial capital letter. I realised that a tick I had placed against a word close to the relevant entry had extended so that it bisected the 'I', making it unclear. Since it had not occurred to me that 'Internet' might be capitalised, from then on I read the entry in the way I had expected to see it, with the initial letter in the lower case. Imagine how I would have felt if this had ultimately made the difference between winning and losing!

I'm not one of those lucky people who have been blessed with a photographic memory. Personally I'm what's known as an auditory learner - I find it easier to remember things I've heard than things I've seen. A good way of reinforcing lists in your memory is to record them onto a dictaphone, and then listen to them as many times as necessary for them to sink in. An advantage of this system is that it's possible to combine aural learning with some other mundane activity, such as ironing, for which you need your eyes but not necessarily your brain. However, I would add that I found listening to lists of words on the dictaphone whilst following them visually extremely useful.

Unfortunately, I thought of the technique of using the dictaphone late in the day, in the run-up to the Champion of Champions series; otherwise I would have used it more extensively. However, I did enough work to realise the importance of setting about the task of recording a list when you have enough time in hand to do it steadily. If you end up gabbling the words, it will be more difficult to take them all on board when you rehear them. Also, when making a recording it is important to speak clearly, and it is a good idea to spell out any words that you might struggle to identify later. If you find that you are getting fed up with the sound of your own voice, you could always ask someone else to do the recording for you.

<u>Techniques for remembering difficult spellings</u>

If you find that you have habitual difficulty remembering how to spell particular words, try using your imagination to come up with a way round the problem. For instance, I used to struggle with the plural of the word 'corgi', which comes up quite regularly on Countdown. I couldn't remember whether you added an 's' to make a six, or '-es' to make a seven. At some point it occurred to me to picture the Queen taking six corgis for a walk. This indicates that the plural has *six* letters in it, so the correct spelling must be 'corgis'.

Another example involves linking words, as detailed above, this time on the basis of equal length when correctly spelt. I used to have difficulty with 'gruesome' (was the 'e' in the middle supposed to be there?) and 'gormless' (was there a 'u' after the 'o'?). Once it dawned on me that both words, when correctly spelt, were eights, my problem was solved and I was never left in a quandary again!

Websites

There is a growing number of websites relating to Countdown, many of which are helpful to those wishing to improve their prowess. I have already mentioned Soo Reams's website www.thecountdowncorral.com in connection with reviews of past programmes. I shall begin with a description of this site's various useful features.

A lot of thought has gone into the compilation of two lists of words: 'sevens which are never the maximum' and 'eights which are always winners'. The former contains around a dozen seven-letter combinations, comprising five consonants and two vowels, not all of which are words in their own right. If you notice any of these combinations you can be sure that there must be at least an eight-letter word in the offing. The reason for this is as follows: since every letters selection has to contain at least three vowels, there must be at least one more vowel among the two letters not used in the combination. What is distinctive about these combinations is that, whichever vowel is added, an eight-letter word can be formed. The list on the website goes on to identify the five possible eights related to the various combinations.

Having decided that this was a very useful list to know, I printed a copy of it and set about constructing some rather nonsensical sentences, as a means of reinforcing the words concerned in my mind. For instance, with regard to the combination '*ginners*' I came up with: 'the **sneering grannies** were **ensuring** the **resining** of the **negronis**'. I recorded these sentences onto the dictaphone, too. I felt silly doing it, but the fact that I was able to pluck the above example from memory when writing this section some weeks later shows that it worked!

The website also features Paul Howe's 'Countgen', an authentic replication of the numbers game. An especially useful feature is that it is linked to a solution-finder at www.crosswordtools.com.

Finally, with regard to www.thecountdowncorral.com, the conundrum challenges are particularly demanding. There are various options, all of which are against the clock: the 'sprint' (three conundrums), the 'challenge' (ten conundrums), the 'expert challenge' (ten difficult conundrums) and the 'marathon' (thirty conundrums). A recent addition is an 'Ode to Countdown', featuring eight conundrums which are allowable on Countdown but would not be acceptable in Scrabble. Details of top performances are displayed after each round you play. If you want to compete with the record-holders you will need not only to spot the solutions straight away, but also to type them very quickly!

Another useful website for developing conundrum-solving skills is www.flashbits.co.uk, which enables you to get a feel for the experience of facing a conundrum on the show. You only attempt one conundrum at a time, and the letters are rearranged in such a way that something vaguely meaningful results. The music plays for thirty seconds, as it would on the programme, and if you haven't got the answer it is then revealed. I rate this even more useful than playing along with the show, because you can play as many times as you like, and there is no other contestant to buzz in after one second and leave you wondering whether you might have seen it given more time!

An especially interesting and informative website is Mike Brown's www.thecountdownpage.com. This gives a wealth of detail about the history of the programme, listing, for instance, champions and celebrities. From a practice point of view, there is an abundance of round-by-round records of past games, the usefulness of which cannot be overstated. The links to www.thecountdownpage.com are particularly comprehensive, enabling access to a wide selection of number and letter generators. One such website is www.kountdown.co.uk. This provides yet more useful practice. However, some of the answers identified by the solution-finders are words that are not listed in the *Oxford Dictionary of English* and would not be acceptable on Countdown.

For those who wish to assess their readiness to pass the audition, and need an indication of what they might expect to achieve if successful, a visit to www.askoxford.com is a must. The sample audition follows the format of a genuine audition, which is slightly different from that used on the programme itself. Would-be contestants are shown how to calculate their score, and how to determine their potential from the resulting total.

Section 4

<u>Conundrums</u>

You often hear contestants on the show saying that they hardly ever get the conundrums. This certainly is the most daunting challenge of the show, being the only one where you are aiming to be the first to buzz in with the correct answer. Often the outcome of the contest is hanging in the balance, which of course makes it even harder. As far as keeping the inevitable apprehension at bay is concerned, there is nothing like justified confidence, stemming from the knowledge that you regularly solve the conundrums at home. This is something which can be acquired, but only through substantial practice.

As mentioned in the section above, access to on-line help can be gained by paying visits to www.thecountdowncorral.com. There are various other ways of developing your conundrum-solving skills and enhancing your familiarity with the words used as conundrums. The Countdown board games and puzzle books contain hundreds of conundrums These can be examined and re-examined until you are familiar with them.

Additionally, you can make up your own conundrums, or ask someone to make them up for you. Making up conundrums is not as hard as you might imagine, and the results can be quite satisfying. If you happen to remember both the product of your efforts, as well as the word you started out with, that's great: if you were lucky enough to come across it on the programme you would recognise it immediately. If, on the other hand, when you come to look back at the product you have no idea what the original word was, then you can use it for the purposes of practice.

As part of my preparation for the Champion of Champions series, I sought to identify words that I thought were likely answers to conundrums appropriate for this level of competition. I had observed from previous series that such words tended to be relatively uncommon, but not so obscure that nobody would recognise the answer. For example, 'protected' or 'wonderful' would probably be too obvious, 'isooctane' or 'psoriatic' too rarefied, while 'enigmatic' or 'negotiate' would be about right. At any rate, the words which form the backbone of the normal conundrum repertoire could definitely be excluded, as it was well known that Damian considered these too easy for the top players. I narrowed the choice down to about 1,000 words, and was able to concoct some sort of conundrum for the majority of them. Of the words I had identified, about half came up during the series, although in each case Damian had composed a different conundrum from the one I had produced!

<u>Helpful hints for making up and solving conundrums</u>

Firstly, it's important to understand that there are some nine-letter words that would never be used as conundrums, and also that there are some conundrums which would rarely or never appear in the letters games. In the former category are words which are basically eights with an 's' on the end (such as 'colanders'), and words which are anagrams of each other (such as 'faithless' and 'flashiest'). In the latter category are words with a consonant/vowel mix that would contravene the rule regarding the 'minimum of three vowels, maximum of five vowels' (for example, 'dragonfly', which has only two vowels). Also in the latter category are words that the letter distribution would effectively preclude (such as 'pineapple' - I can't recall ever seeing three 'p's in one selection).

A good way of making up conundrums to practise on is to set out the nine letters in the form of a grid, as recommended above in the section on letters games. You can use this to experiment with various ways of combining the letters to form bizarre and amusing alternatives to the original word. Here is an example of a nine-letter word from which a considerable number of conundrums can be produced. See how many you can spot. The ones I have come up with can be found in the footnote to this section.

CASHPOINT

or, in grid form:

P A C

H I T

N O S

Once you have compiled some conundrums to use for practice purposes, you may find it useful to put them on pocket-sized pieces of squared paper, with the answer on the other side. If your writing is small, you can fit a number of conundrums on the same square. You can carry some with you, in your pocket or your handbag, and take them out when you are on the bus or the train, or when you are in a queue. It is surprising how much time that would otherwise be completely wasted can be put to good use by doing this. I used squares in this way for nine-letter words which would *not* appear as conundrums as well, with the answer on one side and the letters in the form of a grid on the other. Over the many months of my preparation for my Countdown quest I analysed thousands of words in this way, ending up with a veritable heap of paper squares. It was fun, and a worthwhile endeavour in every way. I don't think I would otherwise have solved 13 of the 15 conundrums I faced on the programme, including four of the five which were crucial!

Once you have sufficient familiarity with the many hundreds of nine-letter words which might be used as conundrums, you may be able to get to the stage where you recognise most of them more or less instantaneously. The ones which might previously have seemed hard can become easy, especially if the combination of letters involved is clearly unique. In my Champion of Champions quarter-final, both Matt Shore and I spotted 'soliloquy' at once. As Matt said to me afterwards, it was difficult to see how it could have been anything else. The nine-letter words which are hardest to spot (whether as conundrums or in the context of ordinary letters games) are those which are too much like other words: 'essential' is one example, 'saintlier' another. I have compiled a list of the 100 nine-letter words which are hardest to spot, which you will find in Appendix 3. If you practise solving these until you recognise them all, you may give yourself a big advantage over your opponent if one of them pops up.

Footnote:

Conundrums in respect of 'Cashpoint': Thiscapon, Topchains, Chainspot, Chopstain, Icantposh, Nothiscap, Hotpanics, Apitchson, Catonship, Ichopants, Sonicpath, Iconspath, Coinspath, Antichops, Itcanshop, Icantshop, Canitshop

Section 5

Numbers games

So many contestants hate the numbers games! Even some series champions like John Mayhew have admitted that it isn't their strongest suit. Carol's advice is 'not to be frightened of the numbers'. Confidence certainly is important, and if you are lucky enough to be a 'natural' when it comes to arithmetic then you shouldn't have any fear of the numbers games. But what if you do find this aspect of the challenge daunting? Is there a way of overcoming that drawback? I believe you can improve through practice.

As almost all solutions to numbers games involve multiplication, knowing your 'times tables' is vital. This includes the 75 times table, which isn't one you would have been instructed to learn at school.

Another important thing to realise is that there are certain clues, which you can obtain from the target figure itself, as to how to go about arriving at a solution. Most of these are fairly easy to assimilate, and often enable a seemingly difficult problem to resolve itself as if by magic!

I'll start with the more obvious points, and work towards the more obscure ones.

Round numbers

When the target is a round number, it will be divisible by both five and ten.

Even when the target is not a round number, having a ten in the selection provides a useful option, as you can try to calculate a nearby round number and then endeavour to find the amount by which it differs from the target. Remember to consider working with a round number *above* the target, as well as below; for example, if the target is 716 you may well have more success trying to find $(10 \times 72) - 4$ than $(10 \times 71) + 4$, because 72 is a multiple of 2, 3, 4, 6, 8, 9, 12, 18, 24 and 36, whereas 71 is a prime number.

Multiples of five

If a target ends in a five, it will be a multiple by five. To find out what number you require from the remainder of the selection, read the first two digits of the target as a two-digit number, double it, and add one. So for example $385 = (38 \times 2) + 1 = 77$.

Multiples of two/doubling the target

At the risk of stating the obvious, any target that is an even number must be divisible by two. This can occasionally be helpful if you have a two in the selection, and are struggling to find a means of arriving at the target. Conversely, you might want to double the target, see if you can arrive at the figure you have created using the remaining numbers, and leave the two aside for the purposes of division to achieve the original target. This can be particularly useful in a situation where the target is an odd number and the selection is dominated by even numbers. The possibility of quadrupling the target in a selection containing a four is worth mentioning, although I can't recall ever having seen anyone do this.

Multiples of nine

Let's begin with an observation that I've heard Carol make a number of times over the years. If the sum of the three digits of the target is either nine or a multiple of nine, then the target must be a multiple of nine. You still have to do the necessary division to arrive at a figure to calculate from the remaining numbers. It is therefore useful to know the three-digit round numbers which are divisible by nine (basically the nine times table with a 0 on the end). You can work from one of the round numbers either side of the target to home in on the number required. For example, you know that 738 is divisible by 9, because $7 + 3 + 8 = 18$. Since 738 is not far away from 720, which you know to be 9×80, you then subtract 720 from 738 to arrive at 18, which you know to be 2×9. You can therefore deduce that $738 = (80 \times 9)$ plus (2×9), which equates to 82×9. If you have a 9 in the selection, you can look to see whether you can make 82 from the remaining numbers. If you haven't got a nine, but can make one, say by adding a four and a five, you may still be able to produce 82 from the remaining numbers.

Multiples of three

Similarly, any number which adds up to three, or a number which is a multiple of three, must be divisible by three. Again, you can use those nearby round numbers which are multiples of three to help you find the number you need to multiply by three to hit the target.

Since nine is a multiple of three, any number exactly divisible by nine will also be exactly divisible by three. (Mathematicians would say that this is an example of the transitive law.)

Multiples of six and eighteen

Any *even number* which is a multiple of three must also be divisible by six.

Any *even number* which is a multiple of nine must also be a multiple of eighteen. This might be useful if, for instance, you don't have a 9 in the selection, but do have a 25, and a 7 which you can subtract from it to arrive at eighteen. To calculate the number you require to multiply by eighteen, find the number you would have needed if you were multiplying by nine and halve it.

Furthermore, since eighteen is a multiple of six, any multiple of eighteen is also a multiple of six, affording you another possible avenue to explore in your search for a solution. (Again, this is due to the operation of the transitive law.)

Returning to the example of 738 above, you can establish that this can be produced by multiplying any of the following combinations 18×41, 9×82, 6×123 and 3×246. Finally, as an even number it is of course divisible by two, offering the further possibility of 369×2.

Multiples of eleven

It is sometimes possible to establish fairly readily that a target is a multiple of eleven. The disadvantage of attempting a solution involving an eleven is that you will have to use at least two numbers to make the eleven, thereby leaving you with a maximum of four others to play with. On the other hand, if you spot that a target is a multiple of eleven it is relatively easy to work out what the other number required in the calculation is.

There are two indications that a three-digit number is a multiple of eleven. If the two outer digits add up to the middle digit, then that number can be calculated by multiplying eleven by whatever number you would be left with if you took out the middle digit altogether. If you find this hard to visualise, you could write out the target in large handwriting and put your finger over the middle digit.

Here's an example: 264 is divisible by 11 because 2 + 4 = 6. If you ignore the 6, you are left with 24, therefore 264 = 11 × 24.

The other indication that a number is a multiple of eleven is when the middle digit is a 0 and the other two digits add up to eleven: for example 209, 308 and 407. To work out the number you need to multiply by eleven in order to arrive at the target, take out the middle digit as described above, but subtract ten from the resulting two-digit number. Hence, for example, 209 = 11 × (29 - 10), that is 11 × 19.

Although these techniques are reliable in the sense that they always work, they do not enable you to identify every target that is a multiple of eleven, as there are some which do not conform to either of the patterns outlined above: for example 319, 418 and 429.

Multiples of 37

Any target featuring three identical digits will be a multiple of 37. Finding out what you need to multiply by 37 is easy: simply add the three digits! So for example 222 = 37 × (2 + 2 + 2), that is 37 × 6. In this instance, if you have a six in the selection, you have five numbers left from which to compute 37. This is just as well, because you will always need at least three of them, owing to the fact that 37 is a prime number and is more than ten away from the nearest large numbers, 25 and 50. A higher target of this type will be harder to achieve, e.g. for 888 (24 x 37) you will need to use at least two numbers to make the 24 and at least three to make the 37.

Relative difficulty of number selections

Turning to the relative merits of the various options available to you when choosing numbers on the programme, there is no doubt that the 'classic selection' (as Carol often calls it) of one large number and five small numbers, is the most likely to enable you to hit the target. Therefore, if you are defending a lead, or aiming for a high score (as opposed to simply winning the game), then you should go for this option. The next easiest selection is 'two large and four small'. There is not much to choose between the remaining options in terms of degree of difficulty. You occasionally find that 'three from the top' or 'four from the top' yield an obvious solution. (Such was the case in the second numbers game in my Champion of Champions final: in an attempt to break the deadlock I went for four large numbers, only to be thwarted when the target turned out to be 175!) However, 'six small numbers' is almost never easy, and can be a good choice if you are proficient with numbers and are behind in the game.

One from the top row

When a selection of 'one large number and five small ones' contains the 100, the target will almost invariably be achievable. Remember to consider working downwards from the round hundred above the target. For example if the target is 867 it may be easier to reduce 900 by 33 than increase 800 by 67 (especially as 900 and 33 are both divisible by 3, affording the possibility of finding 289×3 to arrive at the target).

If the only large number is a 75, the importance of knowing your 75 times table becomes apparent. If you find it hard to remember, try practising with the numbers from the board game (or numbers you've selected randomly yourself), using 75 all the time until it becomes second nature. The multiplication tables taught at school stop at 12, but for Countdown purposes 13 × 75 = 975 is well worth remembering, and even 14 × 75 = 1,050 might come in useful. For example, say you have a target of 994, with a 75 and a 4 in the selection. If you know that 14 x 75 =1,050 and realise that 14 × 4 gives you the 56 you need to subtract in order to arrive at 994, you can deduce that 994 = 14 × (75 - 4), which is 14 × 71. Given that you have the 75 and the 4 required, you just need to make up the 14 from the remaining small numbers, which should almost certainly be possible.

Split multiplication

With selections where the only large number is one of the lower possibilities, i.e. 50 or particularly 25, some degree of multiplication will inevitably be required in the calculation. If you have watched the show regularly, you will surely have seen Carol use the technique of 'split multiplication'. This is where you multiply the large number by one of the small numbers, then adjust the subtotal in some way, before multiplying by another small number to home in on the target.

Here's a relatively simple example: say you have a target of 963, and your only large number is 25. Your small numbers include 4, 7, and 9. A correct solution would be 4 × 25 = 100, plus 7 = 107, multiplied by 9 = 963. The reason that this is a relatively easy solution to spot is that using the 4 to multiply by the 25 to give 100 is something that springs to mind fairly readily.

Now here's a more difficult example: your target is 668, and the large number is again the 25. Your small numbers include 4, 7 and 8. You might try multiplying the 25 by the 4 to give 100 as in the above example; you can multiply this by the 7 to get 700, then work on the 8 and the other two small numbers to make the 32 you require to subtract. Alternatively, you could take the 8 from the 100 you created before you multiply by the 7. This would give you $92 \times 7 = 644$, leaving you needing to find 24 to add to this to make 668. Whether either of these approaches will work depends on what the remaining small numbers in the selection are. A solution is in fact possible using only the numbers I have given, by employing the technique of 'split multiplication'. However, to achieve this you have to go against the grain and start by multiplying the 25 by the 7 to get 175. You can then subtract the 8 to leave 167. Only then do you multiply by the 4 to arrive at 668.

Like so many facets of Countdown, seeing the opportunity to use 'split multiplication' is a matter of practice. You can use the numbers supplied with the board game to work specifically on this aspect of the numbers game. As most of the occasions when the technique is helpful occur when the large number is 25 or 50, pre-select either of these numbers. Arrange the target numbers so that you will be working towards a high target, say 700+, as this will increase the likelihood that split multiplication can come into play.

Practise going against your instincts. For instance, if you have a target of 811, and your selection includes a 50, it is natural to start by figuring that you need to multiply 50 by 16 to get 800. If your selection includes an 8 and a 2, the obvious route to take is to multiply these two numbers together to get the 16. You then try to make the leftover 11 from the remaining numbers. Of course this *may* work. But what if the numbers you are left with are 1, 1 and 6? The best you can achieve is $(1+1) \times 6 = 12$, enabling you to get 812, one off the target. If you have reached this conclusion before the 30 seconds elapses, and you use the rest of the time to continue trying, your next approach is likely to be to multiply the 50 by 2. You then try to add something to the 100 before multiplying by 8, and use the remaining numbers to home in on the target. The best you can achieve by doing this is $(100 + 1 + 1) \times 8$ equals 816, less the 6 equals 810. You are still one away! However, if you multiply the 50 by the 8 to get 400, you can then add the 6 to get 406; you then multiply by 2, to get 812, from which you can subtract 1 to make 811.

The problem is that the method which actually enables you to hit the target is the last one you are likely to consider! So how do you get round this? The key is to remember that when you are multiplying a large number by two smaller numbers you will have two possible subtotals to play around with (in the above example, 100 and 400). I devised a technique which builds a reminder of this into the equation. It involves setting out your workings in an unorthodox manner. As the easiest way to explain it is to demonstrate it, I'll continue with the above example.

Start by writing the target and the selection down as you normally would, so that you have everything you need on the sheet of paper in front of you:

811

50 2   8   6   1   1

Once you have spotted that there is need for 'complex'

multiplication, write down the components like this.

8

50 ×

2

The advantage of doing so is that it encourages you to consider leaving *either* the 8 or the 2 to the second stage of the multiplication, in order to use whichever is required to generate the residual 11 needed to make 811.

The numbers remaining are: 6, 1 and 1.

It becomes relatively easy to see that you can make the 11 by multiplying the 6 by the 2, and subtracting the 1.

You now know that a solution is possible, but you still have to consolidate your workings so that you can explain *how* it is possible.

The fundamental thing to remember is to start by multiplying the large number by the *other* small number - the one you *didn't* use to complete the calculation (in the example this is the 8). If you don't have time to do anything else, draw an arrow between the 50 and the 8 so that you know where to start. The rest of the calculation is likely to fall into place when you come to make your explanation. Of course, if you are playing 'for real', and you haven't written your answer down in full, it is important to say so when making your declaration.

If you do have time to write down your explanation, you obviously begin with the initial multiplication (in this example 8 × 50), then adjust the subtotal (in this instance, by adding the 6 to the 400 you have calculated), before applying the second stage of multiplication (here multiplying 406 by 2) and finally making whatever adjustment may be required (in this case subtracting the 1).

Hence a completed solution to the above example would look like this:

$8 \times 50 = 400$

$400 + 6 = 406$

$406 \times 2 = 812$

$812 - 1 = 811$

One further point to make about the 'classic selection': although the large number is *likely* to be helpful, don't rule out the possibility of coming up with a solution which ignores it.

<u>Two from the top row</u>

Moving on to the relatively rarely used 'two large numbers and four small ones', much of the advice appropriate to the 'classic selection' applies. The most useful tip I know of, which is specific to this selection, is to consider the additional flexibility afforded by the extra large number. Avoid the temptation to consider the two large numbers as *alternatives*, for use in conjunction with the four small numbers. Remember that you can add the two large numbers, subtract one from the other, or divide one into the other to form an additional small number. Conceivably, you might want to multiply one by the other. I recommend making a note of what the outcomes of adding, subtracting and dividing the two large numbers will be, as soon as they appear. There are only six combinations of large numbers (100 and 75, 100 and 50, 100 and 25, 75 and 50, 75 and 25, and 50 and 25). With practice you will find that you recognise the possibilities immediately, so that evaluating them takes no longer than is required for Cecil (the Countdown computer) to come up with a target figure. Knowledge of the 125, 150, and 175 times tables can be useful.

<u>Three from the top row</u>

A selection comprising three large numbers and three small is a good choice if you are competent with numbers but do not feel confident about using the more sophisticated techniques that might come into play when choosing 'four from the top row', as described below. As with selections involving two large numbers, there is scope for addition, subtraction and division of the large numbers prior to incorporating the small numbers into the equation. The presence of the third large number means that the 200 and 225 times tables might additionally come in useful.

Because of the array of possible ways of manipulating the large numbers, it would be too time-consuming to try and calculate them all before proceeding (as recommended above for 'two from the top'). What is important is to have an awareness of what you *might* want to do with the large numbers. For instance, if you have a 25 and a 75 in the selection you know that you can create a round 100 if necessary.

Here's an example of the processes involved in arriving at a solution to a difficult numbers game featuring 'three from the top':

Large numbers: 100, 75, and 25

Small numbers: 5, 6, and 9

Target: 996

The first thing you are likely to notice is that you have a 9 and a 100, which you could multiply. You could then add the 75 and the 25, to make 1,000, and subtract the 5 to arrive at 995 (one off the target).

You might also notice that 1,000 can be reached by adding the large numbers to make 200 and multiplying by 5. You could then subtract the 9 and add the 6 to make 997 (again, one away).

A way of getting the target exactly is to recognise the alternative of adding the 100 and the 75 to make 175. You could try multiplying by 5 to get 875, but that's still 121 away, and you can see fairly readily that the remaining numbers don't look likely to yield this. On the other hand, if you identify the possibility of multiplying 175 by 6 to get 1,050, you are now 54 away. The remaining numbers might seem unhelpful, but if you realise that you have a 9 left, and that you have just performed a sum involving multiplying by 6, the following solution should fall into place: $(100 + 75 - 9) \times 6 = 996$. Analysing the target at the start of the calculation so that you are aware that 996 is a multiple of 6 is key to exploring the right avenue.

Four from the top row

This selection has yielded some of the most impressive moments in the history of the programme. In series 52 John O'Neill, then aged 16, produced some extraordinary solutions, which left even Carol awestruck. His performances encouraged me to investigate the possibilities of this combination. Some of what follows are my own observations, others derive from the 'Four Large Number

Tips' section of Jerry Humphreys' extremely informative website www.jerryh.pwp.blueyonder.co.uk/countdown, which – among other things - sheds light on how Jono gained and applied his knowledge.

'Four from the top' is an appropriate selection if you are very confident of your abilities with the numbers, particularly if you have taken on board and mastered the techniques described below, and if you suspect that your opponent might not be so strong.

Tactically, this is a good choice if you are trying to reduce your opponent's lead, as the chances that the solution will be easy are less than they are for the selections I have already considered. However, if you are defending a lead it may be better to revert to one of the easier choices, thereby reducing the likelihood that your opponent will outdo you.

If you opt for '4 from the top', you know in advance that your selection will definitely include 25, 50, 75 and 100. Only the two small numbers will vary. Carol habitually puts the small numbers up on the board before the large numbers. So if you have the four large numbers written down already, you will have a few extra seconds in which to contemplate what you might want to do with the small numbers. For example, if you see a 9, you will know that the 'alternative target' technique (see below) is a possibility. If you see two 1s, you will know that your chances of finding a solution are not that great, especially if a high target appears.

By using basic addition of combinations of the large numbers, it is possible to find every multiple of 25 between 125 and 250:

125   (100 + 25) or (75 + 50)

150   (100 + 50)

175   (100 + 75)

200   (100 + 75 +25)

225   (100 + 75 +50)

250   (100 + 75 + 50 +25)

You can also make the following multiples of 25 using the large numbers alone:

275   ({50/25} × 100) + 75

300   (75/25) × 100

350   ({75/25} × 100) + 50, or ({100 + 75}/25) × 50, or (100 + 75) × (50/25)

450   (75/25) × (100 + 50), or ({100 + 50}/25) × 75

500   ({75 + 50}/25) × 100 or (100/25) × (75 + 50)

525   ({75 - 50} × 25) - 100

525   ({75 - 50} × 25) - 100

575   ({100 - 75} × 25) - 50

625   (100 - 75) × 25 or (75 - 50) × 25

675   ({100 - 75} × 25) + 50

725   ({75 - 50} × 25) + 100

It is important to remember that small numbers can be incorporated into the equation at any point. For example, if your target is 281 and one of the small numbers is a 3, you can arrive at your target as follows: (50/25) × (100 + 3) + 75.

There are various other three-digit figures that can be calculated from the four large numbers alone. Not only can this be useful if the figure is itself the target: it can also help if the figure is in the vicinity of the target, because you can use the small numbers to home in on the target.

The equations concerned are as follows:

$146 = (\{50 \times 75\} - 100\} \div 25$

$154 = (\{50 \times 75\} + 100) \div 25$

$197 = (\{50 \times 100\} - 75) \div 25$

$203 = (\{50 \times 100\} + 75) \div 25$

$298 = (\{75 \times 100\} - 50) \div 25$

$302 = (\{75 \times 100\} + 50) \div 25$

There is also a technique for incorporating one or both of the small numbers into the basic equations, so offering you another possible way of arriving at a solution. This is dealt with expertly on Jerry Humphrey's website (detailed above).

Also, there are three two-digit numbers which can be calculated from the four large numbers alone.

These are as follows:

$18 = (\{25 \times 50\} + 100) \div 75$

$34 = (\{25 \times 100\} + 50) \div 75$

$67 = (\{50 \times 100\} + 25) \div 75$

Of course, there are no two-digit targets, but there are plenty which are multiples of the above two-digit numbers, and which may be attainable through calculations incorporating the small numbers.

At first sight it might seem a tall order to expect to remember all the possibilities given above. However, it really is a question of familiarising yourself with them through practice. It is helpful to remember that all the three-digit products are the result of dividing by 25, and all the two-digit ones are the result of dividing by 75.

Other sophisticated techniques which are described in detail on Jerry Humphrey's website are the 'rules of 937 ½' (which can come in handy with very high targets) and the 'alternative targets technique'. The latter involves calculating which of the larger numbers can be added to or subtracted from the target in order to leave an alternative target that is a multiple of 9 or 3 – or, if it is an *even* number, 6.

Six small numbers

Like 'four from the top', this is a selection favoured by those who have a high level of confidence towards the numbers games. Even if you would never take this option yourself, it is worth practising with six small numbers, because your opponent may put you in the position where you have to take on the challenge.

There are 20 small numbers available, two of each of the numbers between 1 and 10. As the numbers appear on the board, speculate as to how you might use them.   For example, if you see two 5s emerge, make a note that you can create a 25 by multiplying them together. Another useful thing to do is to check whether the selection contains a 10. If so, when the target comes up look to see what its first two digits are. Make a note of this two-digit number, as well as the number that is one *above* it, and establish which is more likely to be attainable. Begin by asking whether either is a prime number - if so, the *other* will be more promising. (They can't both be prime numbers, because *one* of them *will* be an even number). If you know your multiplication tables, you will   quickly   acquire   the   habit   of   immediately recognising prime numbers. The problem with trying to incorporate two-digit prime numbers into the equation is that you will almost certainly need to use at least three of the other numbers to create them.

Here's an example involving six small numbers, where the application of this technique provides a ready solution to what seems a difficult problem:

1 9 8 6 2 10   Target 713

Firstly, you note the presence of the 10; you then identify that either 10×71 or 10×72 will give you a figure near the target. Next you recognise that while multiplying by 71 would get closer to the target (3 away instead of 7 away), 71 is a prime number, and much less easy to obtain than 72. You then look for a means of arriving at 72, and spot 9×8. So now you have $10 \times 9 \times 8 = 720$. Finally, you ascertain that the target can be found by subtracting the 6 and the 1.

When attempting solutions involving 'six small numbers', the importance of analysing the target cannot be overstated. Speculative multiplication of the small numbers is unlikely to get you anywhere. If the target is high, and the small numbers are mainly towards the lower end of the range, you may have to settle for working towards a nearby figure, in the hope of securing 7 points to get within 5 of the target, or even 5 points to get within 10.

You might find you have to resort to multiplying most or all of the small numbers together in an attempt to get close. If this is the case, and if one of the numbers is a 1, the most productive use for the 1 is probably to add it to the next lowest number. This is because adding 1 to a low number generates a proportionately greater increase than adding 1 to a high number. For example adding 1 to 4 is a 25% increase, whereas adding 1 to 5 is only a 20% increase. This will be reflected in the multiplication potential of the numbers concerned. For example, if your small numbers are 3, 1, 5, 2, 7 and 3 and your target is 951, the best you can achieve is $(1+2) \times 3 \times 3 \times 5 \times 7 = 945$. Adding the 1 anywhere else in the equation will produce a smaller total.

If you have the number 1 twice in the selection and are looking for the highest number you can achieve, add 1+ 1 and multiply the resulting 2 by the rest of the numbers.

Occasionally a high target may be completely impossible to achieve, and for this reason it is a risky choice if you are trying to close a gap on an opponent. 'Four from the top' might represent a better option in this respect, as you will almost always be able to get somewhere near the target.

A recommended approach to numbers games

When it comes to the numbers games, not only is quick thinking essential; it is important to spend every second productively. That's why I recommend having a methodical approach involving three steps, as follows:

1) As soon as the numbers start to appear, begin to think what you *might* want to do with them. When the target comes up, look to see if there is an obvious solution. Be alert for any extraneous clues, such as a groan from the audience, or a lack of activity on the part of your opponent. Make sure you don't attempt anything complicated when the answer is staring you in the face! If you have a solution, write it down carefully, and check your workings until you are absolutely

sure you are right. If you have not seen a solution within the first few seconds of the thirty, move on to step 2.

2) Look to see what clues you can pick up from the target itself with regard to multiplication. For example, if the target is 336, you can deduce that since $3 + 3 + 6 = 12$, and 12 is a multiple of 3, the target must be divisible by 3. So you can ascertain that 112×3 is a possibility. Since 336 is an even number it must be divisible by 6. Therefore you might want to look for 56×6. As long as both halves of the equation are even numbers, you can halve one and double the other to create further possibilities: 28×12, 14×24 and 7×48. You can in fact break these down further in a way which might prove particularly helpful if you are working with six small numbers:

$6 \times 7 \times 8$

or $2 \times 4 \times 6 \times 7$

or even $2 \times 2 \times 3 \times 4 \times 7$

Other possibilities you might notice include: 8×42, 4×84 and 2×168.

In this example there are so many ways that you might go about seeking a solution that if you concentrated on identifying all of them you would be in danger of allowing the time to expire before you'd even begun considering them! The trick is to recognise a promising avenue, explore it and, with luck, come up with a means of hitting the target.

To continue with the example target of 336, suppose your only large number is the 25. In this case 12×28 would be highly likely to produce a solution - particularly if you have a 3 to add to the 25, as you would then have four other small numbers from which to make the 12. Another strong possibility would be to try 14×24, especially if you have a 1 which you could subtract from the 25. If you've found time to identify both these possibilities and explore them, you would be most unlucky not to find an answer.

Of course, not every target is as amenable as 336. Take 337, for example, which is a prime number. 335 yields just one possibility: 5×67. If your target looks unhelpful, or if you have looked at a possibility and then discarded it, move on to step 3.

3) Look to see where the target lies in relation to more easily achievable figures. Remember to look either side of the target for helpful starting points. These will usually be multiples of 25, because the large numbers are all multiples of 25. The most awkward targets in this respect are the groups of four consecutive numbers that are more than ten away from any multiple of 25 (for example 811, 812, 813 and 814 are all more than 10 away from either 800 or 825). Assuming you are able to generate one of the nearby multiples by performing calculations involving one or more large numbers, you will have to use at least two small numbers if you are to home in on the exact number you require. You may find it productive to use the technique of split multiplication described earlier.

Bear in mind that there are numbers other than multiples of 25 that might be considered. Look back at step 2) above and you'll see why 336 is an example. Others include 256, 504, 512 and 576. It's worth knowing why these are useful, so, unless you are already familiar with the reasons, I recommend analysing them in the way I demonstrated above for 336.

As soon as you've found a solution, get it down on paper; spend any remaining time checking that it is correct, and that your workings are clear and legible. If your efforts lead you to a total which isn't spot on, but is within ten of the target, try to avoid writing down your calculations at all if you think you will be able to remember them. Even if you don't think you can recall them unaided, try to write down just enough to jog your memory; for example, note the total you have produced and the starting point for the calculations. If you end up having to go through them, the rest of the calculations are likely to fall into place as you do so. The less time you spend writing down your workings, the more time you will have left to attempt to hit the target exactly. Only if you have taken all the three recommended steps, and you are satisfied that it isn't possible to hit the target exactly, should you consider writing down your workings in full.

Should you see a solution late in the thirty seconds, I recommend making sure that you keep it securely stored in your mind, rather than trying to scribble down something which you may not be able to complete. If you see a means of getting within ten, which you haven't had time to write down, and your opponent declares something closer, keep going over your calculations in your head while your opponent explains theirs - in case they are wrong.

Above all, if you can't find a solution, don't panic. If you have followed the above advice and are still stuck, the chances are that your opponent will be struggling too. As long as the clock is still ticking, persevere! It will almost always be possible to get within ten of the target, and so be in with a chance of scoring some points. If in doubt about whether you are right, declare what you think you have, and find out by working through your calculations with Carol. If you have got it right, that's fine! If you haven't, so what? It will come to light that you've made a mistake, but you'll be

in good company. Dozens of contestants, including top players, have made errors in their calculations. The only reason I got through 45 numbers games without a miscalculation is that I was methodical and remained calm. And the reason I managed to score either 7 or 10 points in 41 of those games was *not* that I am a mathematical genius; I just saw the numbers games as an enjoyable challenge. The many hours I spent practising were both stimulating and rewarding.

Section 6

<u>Staying calm and retaining your composure.</u>

Most people find the thought of appearing on television daunting. Apart from the people I've met through Countdown, everyone I come across seems to say the same thing - they would be far too nervous to do it! With Countdown, not only does your personality come out on national television, but also you are demonstrating the extent of your knowledge and mental capacity in comparison with just one other person. You have no idea who your first - and maybe only - opponent will be, or how good they will be. Unless you can compete with the best, you run the risk of being on the wrong end of a very one-sided scoreline.

Those who have taken on board and implemented all the advice in this book should have the competence required to avoid humiliation. Of course, this will not guarantee success, but the worst you are likely to experience is honourable defeat at the hands of someone who also came well prepared. The confidence that flows from this knowledge has to be the best method of countering nervousness. But what if your ambitions are not intense enough to impel you to go to the lengths required to compete with the top players? You still want to be able to perform to your best ability, even if that just means scoring 50 points instead of 30. The key is to set out to act as you would if you were playing along at home. You have passed an audition; you have therefore already demonstrated that you have the ability required to appear on the show. So just do it again on the programme! Take the view that if your performance is good enough to win, that's a bonus; if it isn't, there's nothing lost, and you will have had an experience that most people will never have.

Once you are actually in the studio, there are several factors that will help you to relax. Firstly, the Countdown backstage team, as well as being highly professional, are very friendly and good-humoured. The experiences you will have backstage will help put you at your ease. What's more, there's no feeling of 'them and us' between the celebrities and the contestants. You will be made to feel that you are an important part of what's happening, as indeed you are! Make the most of the relaxed ambience of the Green Room and take the opportunity to chat with the other contestants over a cup of tea or coffee.

When your turn to take part comes, you will be shown to the studio. Once in your seat you will find that there are plenty of last minute activities to relieve your mind from apprehension: one person will come and give you a microphone to thread through your shirt or blouse; another will perform a sound check; someone else will come and put the final touches to your make-up. You can amuse yourself by watching Dudley the comedian going through his warm-

up routine with the studio audience. Just before the show Carol will come into the studio and join in the banter. The audience is some way from the set, on the other side of the line of cameras, which themselves are not intrusive. The way the studio is set up, along with the focus of the lighting, makes it very easy to cocoon yourself from everything except what is happening on the set itself. Here you will be among people who will seem very familiar to you if you watch the show regularly, and who will be eager to encourage you and put you at your ease. Susie is always complimentary about the words you come up with, even if she has a better one herself. If you are unlucky enough to have difficulty getting off the mark, or you find yourself well behind early on, you will be given reassurance that there is still a long way to go. In the history of the fifteen-round show, no contestant has ever emerged pointless!

The chances are that even if you begin the show feeling nervous, this will ease off as you get engrossed in the game. There will be enough amusing moments and jovial exchanges going on around you to enable the 'fun' side of the experience to overcome the nerves.

Once you have transcended the apprehension, you will be able to compete more effectively. This will engender the confidence required to forget that you are taking part in a televised episode and help you accumulate the same score as you would if you were playing along at home. Should you be fortunate enough to put together a sequence of wins, you will start to get into the routine, and the nerves will disappear. By the time I got to the Champion of Champions final, I felt more relaxed than ever, even though there was a lot at stake. It was this calmness which enabled me to go through some

relatively complicated calculations from memory for the last numbers game, and so advance to a crucial conundrum. Although it still wasn't to be my day, I know without a shadow of doubt that my defeat had nothing to do with a lack of composure on my part. It was entirely due to a superlative performance from an outstanding opponent.

Appendix 1: nine-letter words you must not miss

abolished

abolisher

adipocyte

aitchbone

almonries

alongside

amortised

amortises

anchorite

aphorised

aphorises

arytenoid

assertion/notarises/senoritas

atrophied

atrophies

campesino

caponiers

caponised

caprioles

captioned

catenoids

cavernous

censorial/loniceras

cerastium

charioted

cohabited

cohabiter

comedians/demoniacs

companied

companies

coumarins

countries/cretinous/neurotics

creations/reactions/narcotise/actioners

deflation

delations

depilator

diplomate

dislocate

dominates/staminode

donatives

dovetails

educators/croustade

encomiast

epilators

formalise

genocidal

geomantic

geomatics

ideograms

idolaters/steroidal

incubated

incubator

legations

legionary

lionheads

lionheart

locatives

manicured

manicures

melanotic

morganite

normalise

notarised/derations/ordinates

nursemaid

obligated

obligates

obtainers/baritones

operatics

organised/grandiose/organdies

overpaint

overtrain

palinodes

pantihose

patronise/isopteran

planetoid

polarised

policeman

polyamide

porcelain

precoital

predation

proactive

protamine

randomise/romanised

ravigotes

recoating

redaction

reflation

regionals

relations/orientals/tensorial

reloading/girandole

ruminated

ruminates

scenarios

sealpoint

sectional/coastline

sectorial/sclerotia

solarised

sonicated

sonicates

strobilae

valorised

valorises

vaporised

vectorial

veronicas

vocalised

vocaliser

vocalises

voicemail

Appendix 2: words containing five different consonants and four different vowels

abduction

abjection

ablutions

abolished

abolisher

abruption

abusively

abutilons

acupoints

adipocyte

admixture

advection

aepyornis

aitchbone

almonries

alongside

amortised

amortized

amortizes

amphibole

amplitude

anchorite

anchovies

anguished

anodizers

anorexics

anxiously

aphorised

aphorized

aphorizes

artichoke

arytenoid

atrophied

atrophies

authoring

autowinds

avirulent

avouching

balconied

balconies

bandolier

baritones

barouches	carbonise
baulkiest	carbonize
befouling	carousing
bifurcate	catenoids
binocular	cavernous
bivouacks	ceanothus
bloviated	censorial
bloviates	centurial
bohemians	cerastium
botanised	charioted
botanized	chelation
botanizes	cherimoya
boulevard	cingulate
bounciest	clafoutis
bricolage	cloudiest
bromeliad	clozapine
cabrioles	clupeoids
cabriolet	coevality
calumnies	cohabited
campesino	cohabiter
caponiers	colubrine
caponised	columbine
caponized	columbite
caponizes	combative
caprioles	comedians
capsulize	companied
captioned	companies

configure

conjugate

consulate

copulated

copulates

costumier

coumarins

countable

countries

courantes

courtesan

croupades

croustade

culminate

cuneiform

cunjevois

curations

curatives

curtained

curtilage

cushioned

cuspidate

custodial

custodian

cstomize

dangerous

decimator

delations

demoniacs

dentalium

depilator

detouring

devaluing

deviators

deviously

diaphones

diazotype

diplomate

dipterous

disfavour

dislocate

dogmatise

dogmatize

dominates

donatives

doughiest

doughtier

dovetails

dulcitone

duplicate

durations

eastbound

educators

eductions

emulating

emulators

encomiast

enviously

epidurals

epilators

eruptions

eucryphia

eutrophic

exclusion

excursion

exfoliant

exordiums

expiators

expiatory

expulsion

extrusion

extrusion

factories

factorise

factorize

faculties

farmhouse

fashioned

fashioner

feudality

figurante

filatures

flameouts

flavoured

floriated

floruited

flouncier

fluorides

focalised

focalized

focalizes

forecabin

formalise

formalize

formative

formulaic

formulate

fornicate

fortalice

foundries

fractious

framboise

fruticose

fulminate

fumaroles

fumarolic

fumigated

fumigates

fumigator

furcation

genocidal

geomantic

geomatics

girandole

grandiose

granulite

graticule

guidepost

guideways

habitudes

hailstone

halogenic

harlequin

heinously

heliogram

hexaploid

hideously

hobnailed

hodiernal

housecarl

housemaid

humanised

humanized

humanizes

humanoids

ibuprofen

ideograms

ideograph

ignorable

importune

imposture

impounder

imputable

inclosure

incubated

incubator

inculpate

incurable

incurvate

indecorum

indurates

insourced

insulated

insulator

insurable

isopteran

jargonise

jargonize

jointures

jubilance

jubilated

jubilates

juxtaposekkalsomine

labouring

labourism

labourist

langouste

legionary

lichenous

lifeboats

lifebuoys

lifeguard

ligatured

ligatures

lionheads

lionheart

locatives

longitude

loniceras

loquacity

lubricate

luxations

lagnitude

mailboxes

malthouse

manicured

manicures

manifesto

manucodes

masculine

mediators

mediatory

melanotic

melodicas

metabolic

microwave

misquoted

modulates

moralised

moralized

moralizes

morganite

mosaicked

mouldiest

mountable

mousebird

mousetrap

moustache

mucronate

muishonde

mujahedin

muscadine

muscarine

muscovite

mutagenic

narcotise

narcotize	organdies
naughtier	organised
nectarous	organized
neighbour	organizes
neuralgic	orientals
neuropath	osculated
neuropils	ostracize
neurotics	outbacker
nickelous	outdriven
normalise	outdrives
normalize	outfacing
normative	outfields
notarised	outlawing
notarized	outliners
notarizes	outpacing
noughties	outplayed
nourished	outracing
nursemaid	outranged
obfuscate	outranges
objurgate	outranked
obligated	outrivals
obligates	outsailed
obtainers	outspread
obtrusive	outwalked
ocularist	ovalbumin
operatics	overawing
ordinates	overhauls

overpaint

overusing

overusing

oviductal

ovulating

palinodes

pantihose

parboiled

parhelion

patchouli

paunchier

pecuniary

perfusion

picayunes

pinafores

pishrogue

piteously

pivotable

planetoid

plastique

playhouse

plumerias

pnrumatic

polarised

polarized

polarizes

policeman

polyamide

porcelain

pouchiest

poulticed

poultices

poundages

praiseful

precoital

predation

proactive

probative

proguanil

proscenia

protamine

proximate

ptomaines

pulmonate

pulsation

purgation

purgative

purloined

quagmires

quantiles

quantised

quantiser

quantized

quantizer

quantizes

quartiles

quatorzes

quavering

quickbeam

quodlibet

randomise

randomize

ravigotes

recaption

reclusion

recoating

recouping

refashion

reflation

regionals

rehousing

reloading

repulsion

requalify

requintos

requitals

revaluing

revulsion

righteous

romanised

romanized

romanizes

routinely

royalties

rubicons

ruminated

ruminates

savourily

savouring

sealpoint

sectional

sectorial

semilunar

septarium

shadowier

shogunate

signature

simulated

simulator

siphonage

slouchier

sluiceway

sobriquet

solarized

solmizate

sonicated

spiculate

sporulate

squiredom	touchable
staminode	touchline
steroidal	trapezium
strobilae	trapezius
subalpine	trapezoid
subatomic	triazoles
subdeacon	trigamous
subeditor	troupials
subjoined	truancies
sublation	uitlander
sublimate	umpirages
submarine	unclaimed
subregion	uncloaked
subrogate	undercoat
subtopian	undersoil
suctorial	unethical
superacid	ungodlier
supercoil	uniformed
supernova	unloaders
supinated	unrealism
supinator	unreality
samboured	unwarlike
tambourin	unweights
tamoxifen	upheaving
tediously	uploading
tensorial	urbanised
timeously	urbanized

urbanizes

valorised

valorized

valorizes

vaporised

vaporized

vaporizes

vapouring

vapourish

varicosed

variously

vectorial

vehicular

verminous

versional

vesicular

vexations

viceroyal

videogram

vocalised

vocaliser

vocalized

vocalizer

vocalizes

voidances

volumised

volumized

volumizes

vouchsafe

vulcanised

vulcanized

vulcanizes

vulgarise

vulgarize

womanised

womaniser

womanized

womanizer

womanizes

womanlike

zeugmatic

Appendix 3 – 100 hardest nine-letter words to spot

activated

activates

candlelit

castigate

centesimo

cinematic

deadliest

deathlier

decussate

deistical

demitasse

desiccate

designate

diaconate

disregard

disrepair

distraite

dreariest

engrailed

entertain

epitomist

escapists

essential

estaminet

etiolated

evaginate

implicate

instigate

intensive

intestine

inverters

investors

materials

meliorate

meliorist

metacarpi

metatarsi

mistletoe

negotiant

negotiate

ninetieth

noviciate

novitiate

obstinate

octennial

orientate

originate

perennial

piecemeal

priorates

prussiate

reanimate

reinstate

reiterate

renovated

renovates

repairman

repairmen

repudiate

respirate

restrains

restraint

retailers

retaliate

retinitis

retrieval

saintlier

santolina

santonica

sciential

sensorial

serialism

serialist

seriation

sestertii

sexennial

sirenians

solarised

staircase

stapedial

stapelias

storiated

stromatic

tantivies

tastevins

tectorial

tetanised

tetanises

timescale

trichinae

triennial

valencies

varietals

varietist

ventilate

verminate

vernation

vesicated

vesicates

visagiste

Appendix 4: nine-letter words containing 'i', 'n' and 'g' (other than verb forms ending in '-ing')

abiogenic

aborigine

agitation

agnolotti

agnostics

agronomic

alginates

alongside

amygdalin

analgesia

analgesic

analogies

analogise

analogize

angelfish

angelical

angelicas

angiogram

angiomata

anglicise

anglicize

anilingus

anisogamy

antigenic

aragonite

argentine

ashlaring

athelings

aubergine

autogenic

bangtails

bargained

bargainer

beestings

beginners

bengaline

benighted

benignant

benignity

bergenias

bigeneric

biguanide

bilingual

binturong

bioregion

bogginess

branigans

cardigans

cassingle

centigram

champaign

cingulate

clearwing

cognisant

cognitive

cognizant

collegian

commingle

concierge

condignly

congenial

consigned

consignee

consignor

contagion

dealigned

depigment

designate

diagnosed

diagnoses

diagnosis

digestion

digitalin

diligence

dinginess

diosgenin

divergent

dodginess

emigrants

endogenic

engirdled

engirdles

engrailed

engrained

enlighten

envisaged

envisages

ergonomic

erigerons

eryngiums

espionage

euglenoid

evaginate

evangelic

eveninger

exergonic

feringhis

figurante

figurines

finaglers

fingertip

flamingos

foodgrain

forewings

foundling

frangible

franglais

fumigants

fungicide

fungiform

gabardine

gaberdine

gainsayer

galenical

galingale

gallivant

galvanise

galvanism

galvanize

ganglions

gantlines

gardenias

garnishee

garniture

gaudiness

gaukiness

gauziness

gavelkind

gazillion

geminated

geminates

genetical

genitalia

genitival

genitives

genitures

genocidal

gntility

gomantic

grmanium

grminate

grundive

gsneriad

gestation

giantlike

giddiness

gigantism

ginormous

girandole

gleanings

glissandi

glissando

globulins

gloxinias

glutamine

glutinous

glycerine

gnarliest

goatskins

godliness

gondolier

goniatite

goopiness

gooseskin

gorgonian

gradation

gradience

gradients

grainiest

grainless

ganaries

gandiose

ganitise

ganitize

ganitoid

ganivore

gandsire

ganulite

gapevine

gatineed

gavitons

geenhide

geenmail

gegarine

grenadier

grenadine

gridirons

grievance

grimalkin

griminess

grosgrain

galantine

guanidine

guanosine

guideline

guildsman

guildsmen

gushiness

gustation

gustiness

gymnasium

gynoecium

gyrations

halogenic

hangnails

harbinger

hegemonic

hingeless

hirelings

histogeny

hobgoblin

hooligans

humdinger

hungriest

hygienist

hypogenic

ignitable

ignitrons

ignoblest

ignorable

ignoramus

ignorance

imagineer

imaginers

immigrant

impingers

inaugural	integrant
incognito	integrins
indigence	integrity
indigenes	intergrow
indigents	intrigant
indignant	intrigued
indignity	intriguer
indraught	intrigues
indulgent	inveigled
indulgers	inveigles
inelegant	isangomas
infringed	isinyanga
infringer	izimbongi
infringes	iangliest
ingathers	jingoists
ingenuity	jungliest
ingestion	kingsides
inglenook	lamington
ingrafted	languidly
ingrained	legations
inselberg	legionary
insurgent	lengthier
inswinger	lightened
intaglios	lignified
integrate	lignifies
integrals	lilangeni
integrand	lingerers

linguists	marginate
litigants	menagerie
logicians	meningeal
longevity	menologia
longhairs	meringue
longicorn	metheglin
longitude	misgovern
longliner	mitogenic
longlines	monogenic
losingest	moonlight
louringly	morganite
magazines	mugginess
magicians	mutagenic
magnesian	myoglobin
magnesite	nannygais
magnesium	narghiles
magnetise	naughtier
magnetite	naughtily
magnetize	navigated
magnifico	navigates
magnified	negations
magnifier	negatived
malignant	negatives
malingers	negotiant
manganite	negotiate
margarine	neighbour
marginals	neologise

neologism

neologist

neologize

neuralgia

neuralgic

neuroglia

nightmare

nightwear

nigritude

nostalgia

nostalgic

nurseling

omnirange

oncogenic

oogenesis

organdies

organised

organiser

organises

organists

organized

organizer

organizes

organzine

originals

originate

paganised

paganises

paganized

paganized

paganizes

paginated

paginates

panegyric

pangolins

parawings

pedogenic

peignoirs

peregrine

pleadings

podginess

poignance

poignancy

polygenic

porringer

progestin

prognoses

prognosis

proguanil

ptarmigan

pudginess

pyrogenic

ranginess

realigned

rconsign
redingote
regionals
religions
resignals
rigadoons
rigidness
ringdoves
ringleted
ringsider
ringsides
ringtails
ringtones
rogations
sabrewing
sangfroid
sangrails
sanguines
screeding
scungiest
scungille
scungilli
seafaring
searingly
seedlings
seigneurs
seigneury

seigniors
seigniory
shanghais
shaveling
sheadings
shealings
shearling
sheathing
shielings
shrinkage
signalise
signalize
signaller
signalman
signalmen
signaries
signature
signboard
signified
signifier
signifies
signories
signorina
silvering
siphonage
sitatunga
skijoring

slangiest	unaligned
smidgeons	underling
soaringly	underwing
soigneurs	unweighed
southings	unweights
sovereign	urolagnia
spanglier	vaginally
spongiest	vaginitis
springier	vaginosis
steadings	vainglory
stenosing	vigilance
stingaree	vigilante
stingiest	vintagers
stringier	viologens
surcingle	virginals
swingboat	weaklings
syngeneic	wendigoes
syringeal	whingiest
tanginess	windigoes
tangliest	wingbeats
toxigenic	wingovers
tragedian	woodgrain
triangles	yearlings

Appendix 5: words ending in '–ing' which can be pluralised

airing

arising

beading

briefing

caning

clearing

coaming

covering

coving

craving

croning

cutting

dealing

doing

earning

easting

facing

filing

fining

fluting

footing

gearing

gleaning

heading

hearing

holding

incoming

lacing

leaning

leaving

loaning

malting

moulding

mowing

musing

northing

nosing

outgoing

paling

paring

peeling

piercing

placing

pleading

railing

ranting

reading

reeding

rubbing

ruling

sailing

salting

seeding

seizing

sending

sheading

shealing

shieling

sifting

sounding

southing

steading

taking

tasting

titling

warning

westing

wilding

witling

winding

working

writing

Appendix 6: words ending in '-icide'

algicide

aphicide

biocide

deicide

ethnocide

feticide

filicide

fungicide

genocide

germicide

herbicide

matricide

parricide

patricide

regicide

suicide

uxoricide

vermicide

Appendix 7: words ending in '-ology'

aerology

aetiology

algology

areology

astrology

carpology

cereology

chaology

doxology

ecology

ethnology

ethology

etymology

garbology

hierology

histology

ideology

kidology

limnology

lithology

mereology

metrology

museology

necrology

nephology

neurology

oncology

ontology

pathology

penology

petrology

philology

rheology

scatology

serology

sexology

tautology

teleology

tetralogy

theology

tribology

ufology

xnology

Appendix 8: words ending in '-head'

arrowhead

baldhead

beachhead

bedhead

blackhead

bluehead

bonehead

boofhead

bowhead

breadhead

bulkhead

bullhead

conehead

crackhead

dickhead

drophead

drumhead

duckhead

dumbhead

fathead

flathead

forehead

fuckhead (vulgar)

godhead

lionhead

lunkhead

masthead

mophead

overhead

pinhead

pisshead (vulgar)

pithead

pothead

printhead

raghead

railhead

redhead

skinhead

slaphead

sorehead

spearhead

stairhead

teahead

thickhead

towelhead (offensive)

warhead

Appendix 9: words ending in '-board'

chipboard

clapboard

clipboard

dashboard

footboard

fretboard

garboard

hardboard

headboard

keyboard

kneeboard

larboard (adjective)

leeboard (adjective)

longboard

millboard

mopboard

outboard

pegboard

plugboard

sailboard

seaboard

shipboard

sideboard

signboard

snowboard

starboard (adjective)

surfboard

tailboard

wallboard

washboard

Appendix 10: words ending in '-line'

(unless otherwise stated, all words are nouns which can be pluralised)

airline

backline

baseline

bloodline

bodyline

bowline

breadline

bustline

chatline

coastline

cutline

dateline

deadline

dragline

driveline

eyeline

flatline (verb)

gantline

guideline

hairline

headline (noun/verb)

hemline

hotline

jawline

landline

lifeline

lipline

longline

mainline (verb)

midline

neckline

outline (noun/verb)

punchline

ratlines (plural noun)

shoreline

sideline (noun/verb)

storyline

strapline

tideline

timeline

touchline

towline

tramline

trapline

tumpline

waistline

waterline

Appendix 11: surnames

bezant

bluchers

bogart

bolivar

bonham

brougham

burley

burton

cardigan

cavendish

cooper

dalton

davenport

dexter

dickens

fletcher

fuller

glover

hooper

lambert

macintosh

martin

maxwell

nelson

newton

oersted

palmer

pascal

pelham

ridley

sander

siemens

smetana (mass noun)

smith (noun/verb)

spencer

talbot

thorp(e)   trudgen

tilbury   walker

trilby

Appendix 12: 'names' – words which *sound like* someone's name

adipate   juneberry

allanite   leeward

alsike/s   markhor

amyloid   micrite

anilingus   militate

annalist   patball

colloid   patly

crispate   polymeric

cristate   rickshaw

dentate   ricochet

dictate   soubrette

dimeric   spikemoss

frankly   student

garryowen   sylvinite

gestate

jaywalker

About the author:

Mark Tournoff was born in Aldershot, Hampshire in 1962. He was educated at Lord Wandsworth College, near Basingstoke. He studied Theology at Exeter University, and later Management Accountancy at Croydon Business School. He has worked in the Civil Service, the Health Service, and the transport industry. He has travelled extensively within the United Kingdom and on the continent. His decision to become a novelist was inspired by a course of study with 'The Writing College'. Mark has published two novels under the imprint of Forestdale Publications: "A Nightmare in *Paradise*" (2003) (ISBN 0-9545072-0-7), a mysterious futuristic thriller set in the Sussex countryside; and "Sharp Right to Oblivion" (2007) (ISBN 0-9545072-1-5), a tale of love and betrayal set in Cornwall.

Following his successful appearances on *Countdown* and *Brainteaser* he now gives presentations about his experiences to groups and societies. Mark also provides tuition to children in English and Maths, and teaches English to adult speakers of other languages. His interests include playing the flute in the Croydon Symphonic Band, singing, golf and badminton. He has previously written flute music, songs, sketches and short stories.